CARING FOR OL

CATS & DOGS

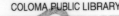

D0563169

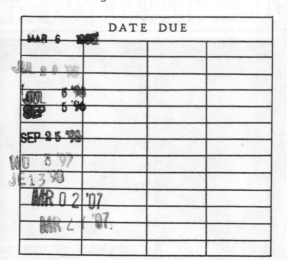

LIFE

ROBERT ANDERSON, DVM & BARBARA WREDE

WILLIAMSON PUBLISHING CHARLOTTE, VERMONT 05445

**Library of Congress
Cataloging-in-Publication Data**

Anderson, Robert, 1943-
Caring for older cats & dogs / by Robert Anderson
and Barbara J. Wrede.
    p. ca.
  ISBN 0-913589-46-2 : $10.95
  1. Dogs. 2. Cats. 3. Dogs—Health. 4. Cats—Health.
5.
Veterinary geriatrics. I. Wrede, Barbara J., 1931- .
II. Title. III. Title: Caring for older cats and dogs.
SF427.A67 1990
636.7'089897—dc20

Cover design: Trezzo-Braren Studio
Illustrator: William P. Hamilton
Typography: Sant Bani Press
Printer: Capital City Press

Williamson Publishing Co.
Charlotte, Vermont 05445

Manufactured in the United States of America

10 9 8 7 6 5 4 3 2

CONTENTS

PREFACE _____ v

Chapter 1 _____ 1
WHAT IS OLD?

Chapter 2 _____ 17
YOU, YOUR PET, AND YOUR VET

Chapter 3 _____ 31
HEALTH PROBLEMS

Chapter 4 _____ 67
ENHANCING THE HOME ENVIRONMENT

Chapter 5 _____ 85
NUTRITION

Chapter 6 _____ 103
POLLUTION AND POISONS

Chapter 7 _____ 119
UNORTHODOX THERAPIES

Chapter 8 _____ 129
KNOWING WHEN IT'S THE END

Chapter 9 _____ 139
PREPARING YOUR NEW PET FOR OLD AGE

APPENDIX _____ 161

INDEX _____ 163

*This book is dedicated
to all those wonderful cats and dogs
who have made our lives richer and fuller.*

—— ACKNOWLEDGEMENTS ——

I've been extremely lucky to know wonderful dog people who have given generously of their time and knowledge. My lifelong thanks go to people like "Deck" Deckrosh, Tony and Eileen Perreault, and others who shared with me their dog lore so that I could share it with you.

My best cat guide has been Deb Stomberg, of Minneapolis, who raised champion Persians and taught me much of what I know about cats.

Most especially I want to thank Dr. George Browne, formerly of Ferndale, California, who, until his death in May of 1987, was the veterinarian who took care of my Great Danes and taught me in a way that goes far beyond simple textbook knowledge. Much of what I pass on here came from Dr. Browne.

There have been other excellent veterinarians in my life, including my coauthor, from whom I've learned many things during our writing of this book.

In truth, my dogs have generally had much better medical care available to them than I have, and I've had a lot more confidence in the veterinarians I've taken my pets to than I've had in most of the doctors I've taken myself to.

Barbara J. Wrede

child, her family raised cocker spaniels, the last of whom died when she was a junior in college. Cockers were followed by boxers, a breed that are among the most humor-loving dogs. As an adult, she spent several years in the company of weimaraners, those ghosty gray and so intelligent German hunting dogs.

As time went by, she found that the weimaraners demanded a stronger disciplinary hand than she preferred to use on dogs, and she phased out of weimaraners and into Great Danes. They have been the constant companions of her and her husband, Kent, for more than twenty years.

Her family includes many cats, too. She began with two six-month-old domestic shorthair kittens she had flown from Connecticut to Fortuna, California, when she moved there in 1964. Today they have the Old Auntie cats, Squeaker and Julia Child who disapprove of all kittens who cross their doorstep; Sally Ride, who goes where she wants to go, and an assortment of her offspring.

Because they have raised many Danes and have been very serious in their promise to people who bought puppies from them that they would be available for consultation throughout the life of the dogs, Barbara and Kent have multiplied their canine experiences far beyond just the dogs they have had at home. The benefits of all these experiences are distilled here for you. The hard part of knowing all these dogs right through their last days is part of what's made the book at times so difficult to write.

On the medical and nutritional aspects of caring for your aging pet in an optimum way, Dr. Anderson, DVM, brings to the book a deep knowledge of and interest in holistic, natural medicine. Bob considers it vitally important that people pay better attention to their dogs' diets. He also believes that people need to take a more preventive approach to sickness. Time and again he emphasizes that early intervention is not only preferable to late, heroic efforts, but it is also less stressful on the pet and likely to produce a better outcome.

Dr. Anderson was graduated from Kansas State University in 1967. His first veterinary practice was in Iowa City, Iowa. A few years after his graduation, Bob moved to northern California. There his first practice was in conjunction with one of the

PREFACE

This has been an instructive and a difficult book to write. The difficult part is that in dealing with the problems and challenges of old or aging pets, we've been visited by the ghosts of all the pets we've lost over the years. That today's veterinary medicine is advanced enough to make some of those past losses unnecessary has made them all the more grievous, but it's also given us cheer to know that our old pets of today have more good years available to them just because of those advances.

The instructive part of this enterprise comes from having two people of different expertise combining their knowledge and experience to get a whole view. Each of us knows things the other didn't until we wrote this book.

This book is a collaboration between two people who have chosen pets as a large part of their professional and personal lives. We are Robert Anderson, a doctor of veterinary medicine, and Barbara J. Wrede, a long-time breeder of purebred dogs. Together we bring many years of experience and expertise to the subject of how you can best care for your aging pets.

Barbara has either been in a family that raised dogs or raised dogs herself for half a century. When she was a small most respected veterinarians in the state, Dr. Stu Fuller, who was widely known for his excellent research. Bob has his own practice in Fortuna, California.

He has raised border collies, those solid, sensible working dogs. Like Barbara, Bob has always had dogs as part of his life. He also has a keen interest in birds, and the resident parrot at his veterinary hospital comments liberally on everything.

As is true when any two experts discuss a subject, Bob and Barbara did not begin with a total meeting of the minds. Bob is the more scientific and clinical of the two. He's cautious, as befits a good diagnostician. If it hasn't been proven, Bob isn't going to make wild claims. Barbara, on the other hand, is more likely to give you anecdotal evidence and to be ready to try new theories if they're benign.

However, Barbara isn't the one you'd take your pet to if you were in deep trouble—Bob is. And as this book has taken shape, the two minds have met. Bob's expertise is so evident that he has never needed to "pull rank." When he explains how things ought to be, a sensible person who cares about the best for pets listens. Barbara's questions have caused Bob to clarify and define what he really believes about many aspects of pet care, bringing him to a stronger than ever commitment to sound preventive medicine as the basis for good pet health.

Between the two, you have one very well-rounded guide.

This book is not intended to replace your relationship with your veterinarian. Neither of us can diagnose your pet through some crystal ball, nor can we prescribe for an individual pet sight unseen. We're giving you the big picture, with an overview of what the aging process entails for your pets. The stories we tell and the examples we give are for your guidance in understanding the range of possibilities as you become more aware of what faces your older pets. Just as no two individuals are exactly alike in every aspect of their sickness or wellness, so also no two pets are exactly alike. That's why medicine, be it human or veterinary, is both a science and an art, while the repair of our cars and our computers is technology, mechanical and straightforward to diagnose. Medicine has vastly more variables.

The suggestions we give you for enhancing your home environment to make life easier for an older pet are things that have worked for us and others. What we're aiming for is basically a guide, a collection of information and strategies you can translate into your own lives and into the lives of your pets. Everybody will tell you how to take care of a puppy or a kitten. We're concerned that you have some help making life longer, better, and more comfortable for that faithful old cat or dog with whom you've been sharing the past many years.

CHAPTER 1

What Is Old?

He was fourteen years old and he ruled his roost regally. True, his walk was slow, but you could also call it stately. All the younger Great Danes in his family knew that when The Boss wanted something, common sense said "Give it to him."

Champion Black Duke of Westwood, the great sire of many excellent Great Danes, teaches us much about not jumping to conclusions when we consider the term "old" as it applies to our pets.

"When you pat him, do it gently," Kay, his owner, said. "He doesn't have too many places left where he doesn't hurt if you touch too hard, but he's still enjoying life, and that's what matters to us."

Indeed Duke was enjoying his life. He was first to greet visitors at the door, posed gravely to be duly admired—and he was a dog to admire—and settled in on his innerspring mattress next to the fireplace when people gathered in the living room.

Fourteen isn't old for some breeds of dogs. For Great Danes, fourteen is nearly record-breaking, and fourteen in basically

1

good health is outstanding. Kay uttered the magic words: "He's still enjoying life."

Duke was no basket case, drooling and shivering in a corner, knowing or caring nothing about what was going on in the world around him. He raised the alarm when visitors came to his house, he made himself available for the social niceties, he ate well, and he took stately strolls around the place, checking up on whatever needed checking up on.

Enjoying life. That's the key when we ponder life and longevity.

Tiger Paws, an old tiger cat, hunted the birds well into his sixteenth year. True, it was an ineffectual hunt, as Tiger was a meat loaf cat, and his sides hung over the branches he sprawled on, waiting for brain-damaged birds to wander blindly into his grasp. But he was still doing what he'd always done, albeit with diminished results. He knew where his food dish was, and where the warm places were in the house. When he gave up his hunting, the end came quickly. He lost all interest in life.

Provide Comfort

There are strategies for making old age as comfortable as possible for your pet. Further, although diseases are more pronounced in old age than at any other time in a pet's life, there are also ways that you, with the cooperation of your trusted veterinarian, can palliate, or ease, the diseased state.

The bad news is that no one can stop the clock of life. It runs, and every living being has its own unique life span. Despite all the love and care in the world, every pet grows old, and none of us can change that hard fact. We humans seem to be the only species that worries about our own—and our pets'—mortality. We need to bear in mind that when we look at an aging pet and worry about how much longer we'll have our old friend around, our pet isn't sharing that worry. Remember that Duke was enjoying his life, and Tiger Paws was a happy meat loaf until perhaps two days or so before his demise.

Probably all pet owners at some time anthropomorphize their pets—that is, we think of them as having the thoughts, feelings, and behaviors of humans. The verdict hasn't been reached on exactly how much animals think, plan, or connive. Just what their feelings of family loyalty are, to their own offspring and to their human families, still isn't agreed on. But we can be fairly certain that many of the human traits, such as worry about impending death, that we project onto our pets exist more in our own minds than in our pets' minds.

Anthropomorphizing is a harmless and generally pleasant pastime. It becomes counterproductive if it interferes with owners getting to observe what is really going on with a pet.

For instance, we saw an elderly poodle who was sick because he was getting insufficient nutrition from an inappropriate diet. His owner was advised to change his pet's diet, incorporating a good-quality kibble for fiber, bulk, and roughage, into his daily intake.

"But his feelings would be hurt," his owner wailed. "I've made him his liver and carrot stew all his life. What would he think if I suddenly stopped treating him so well?"

As a matter of fact, the poor dog might have felt better

physically had he eaten a balanced diet. He might have felt better even mentally had he been able to move his bowels regularly, instead of having to take medication because of his diet. The one thing that poodle won't do is brood about what he's done to fall out of favor with his misguided owner.

Anthropomorphizing needs to be held within reasonable limits. Yes, your cat may be upset at visiting the veterinary office. There are strange smells there—even dog smells. It's alien turf. Only your cheerful reassurance that everything will come out all right is going to calm your pet. And yes, your pet is frightened when it's hurt. Your job is to minimize that fear while you get professional help as fast as you can. The fear is very real and can play a negative role in an animal's recovery from injury or disease.

Our job as pet owners and advocates is to separate our own fears from those of our pets. In the face of our own fears and guilts, we need to be able to become clearheaded, straight thinkers during crisis times when only our good reporting can contribute to a pet's treatment and recovery. After we've helped cope with a crisis, we can fall apart if necessary.

And, of course, every crisis with an aging pet is harder on us as owners than if the pet were younger and stronger, because somewhere in the back of our minds, that clock is ticking inexorably.

——— SIGNS OF OLD AGE ———

What do we mean by "signs of old age?" These are really early symptoms of disease. In the aging process, microscopic changes occur first in tissues. As they increase, the changes become more obvious. Tissue dehydration and fibrosis (an increase in the size and number of fibers in the tissue) are two of the microscopic changes which commonly occur with age. Stiffness, caused by dryness and more fibrous tissues in the area of the joints, is an early indication of arthritis. It may come as the joints get more wear and tear on their surfaces and as the lubricating fluid within the joint decreases in volume.

The same process also occurs in other organ systems. The skin, which is the mirror of the internal body, is one of the first areas to show signs of change. Hair tends to dry and lose its luster. The skin gets flaky, which indicates a lack of moisture in the upper layers of the epidermis.

Treatment for these can begin even before any changes are observed. Some of these changes can be picked up in a pet's annual physical examination. Your veterinarian can see things with the microscope and lab tests that can't be seen by the unaided eye. Nutritional changes, environmental changes, and more natural therapies can be very effectively used to delay the aging process. As the process continues, the measures used to counteract it must become more aggressive. At some point all efforts will cease to benefit the animal—that clock again.

What Is 'Normal' Old Age?

The aging process is a normal stage of life, best described as that time in a living being's existence when deterioration is taking place at a faster rate than regeneration, or repair. The equilibrium between damage and repair, between growth and dying, is tipped to the downward end of the scale.

There are commonly accepted rates of deterioration. We don't expect, for instance, to be as limber ourselves at eighty as we were at twenty. Some sports make such major demands on the body that a player is "old" in the mid-thirties, while others can still be enjoyed by people in their sixties and seventies.

In normal aging, the functions of the bodies of pets slow down. Digestion, for instance, begins to take longer than it did, but it's still going on, and at a normal rate for the age of the individual. The structures of the body start to deteriorate. Broken bones take longer to heal in an older animal. Cuts may be slower to heal. Regeneration is still taking place, but at an increasingly slower rate.

Our goal in pets is to slow the rate of degeneration to the minimum. We must expect that ultimately we'll reach a point where we're losing. But we can rejoice in knowing that before that time comes, we can do much to enable our pets to live as long as possible in as comfortable a state as is humanly possible to provide.

Ideally, onset of the period thought of as old is delayed as long as possible, and during it, the pet is kept as healthy as possible. Pet owners can influence this by providing a proper diet and environment. However, genetic blueprints are an influence in aging that the pet owner cannot reverse. That your English bulldog is older at age ten than your friend's fox terrier is something you can do nothing about. The two breeds age at different rates. But if your English bulldog is younger at age ten than your friend's dog of the same breed, you've probably been providing something extra as you've cared for your pet through the years.

As with people, there are healthy old pets, and there are sickly old ones. Some causes of this you can help. Some you can do little about.

Cats do not present as many problems during the aging process as dogs do. For most cats, the major health problems occur during kittenhood. Once you get a kitten successfully through to adulthood, good care and proper diet will give your cat many, many years of vigorous health. People who have lived with cats and dogs know that the fifteen-year-old cat seldom presents many health problems, while most fifteen-year-old dogs are showing one or more signs of deterioration.

When to Intervene

The point at which we intervene in our pets' health processes depends on our own awareness that change is occurring. This depends, too, partly on our ability or our veterinarian's awareness and ability to observe and make changes. The changes should be as early as possible so they can be as gentle as possible.

Think about that elderly poodle. Had his owner been willing to listen to the veterinarian years ago, she wouldn't have had a sickly, constipated dog with rotting teeth and a miserable disposition. Nor would she have had, a year later, a dog that had to be euthanized.

Another factor that influences when we intervene in our pets' health processes is the very nature of the pet itself. There are pets that we can describe as "easy keepers." They fairly burst with vitality. They get their regular immunizations, but other than that, they're never sick. They're ready for a game of ball, a romp at the river, a ride in the car, a roll in catnip— whatever pleasure we and life offer them. They go on, year in and year out, and we have to ask ourselves, "Is Spot nine years old or ten?" These are the pets that get to be ten or twelve years old without ever needing to be seen by a veterinarian except for routine shots.

Veterinarians know that when they see such a pet for the

first time at such an age, there's probably only a short time left for the animal. It's as if these "easy keepers" live life fully and joyously, then one day are old and finished with life. This is especially true with cats. These are the pets that, one morning, we find fast asleep, we think, but actually they are dead.

Conversely, there are the chronically sick ones—never so sick that we despair of them, but never full of bounce and joy. These pets spend much of their time visiting the veterinarian.

One woman named her cat Doctor, because, she said, wherever she and her cat moved around the country, the first thing that cat found out about the new neighborhood was the location of the closest veterinary hospital. Such pets often live more years than the vital ones, and we won't make value judgments on whether they live better or worse lives.

Suddenly They're Old

We all keep track of our own birthdays. We know the ages of our children and guess fairly accurately how old our parents are. But the dog who was a puppy just last year—or so it seems—and the cat that was a kitten so recently often move on into the senior pet status without our noticing. Then suddenly some event causes us to add up the years and say with surprise, "Has it been that long?"

A current favorite Great Dane reminded us that he isn't the silly puppy we've known for years. A fine female Dane came for her breeding appointment, but Pinocchio, the harlequin Dane, simply didn't have the strength in his back legs to get the breeding done. His spirit was willing, but his body played him false.

For a dog who has never before made a clumsy move and who is as silly as he's always been, his lack of stamina came as an unwelcome newsletter from the future, causing us to check his vital statistics and discover that the "puppy" will be nine years old next month. A surprise like this makes an owner aware that some extra attentions must be paid to a pet's diet, his exercise program, and the stresses in his life.

Some Danes have shown age earlier than Pinocchio, and some have held together longer than he. The point is that the one event, that hoped-for breeding, caused a re-examination of just how old Pinocchio was getting to be in terms of his life clock. Suddenly extra attention must be paid to the strategies necessary to extend his life at as high a quality of health and well-being as possible. That's what this book is all about—being sensitive to our pets' aging process and adjusting their lives so they can enjoy their old age.

Cats' Life Span

Various breeds of cats seem to age at about the same rate. They generally have a longer life span than dogs before they show signs of age. You can expect that the years from one to ten will be healthy adult years, unmarked by premature aging. However, the trade-off is that cats have a shorter "old" span to their lives. We seldom see an arthritic old cat, though we see lots of arthritic old dogs. Older cats' teeth and their kidneys are the most vulnerable points. Generally, we don't look regularly at our cats' teeth, and chronic kidney disease comes on so slowly that we don't notice the early changes.

Although different breeds of cats are marked by coat length, color, and quality, as well as by body style—long and slender for the Abyssinian, for instance, as contrasted to chunky and solid for the Maine coon cat—cats do not diverge radically from what one might consider an average body style, size, or shape. Thus it is easier to generalize about cats' rate of aging than it is about dogs'.

Size and Aging

If the average dog is similar in size and shape to the coyote—that is, about thirty pounds in weight and with a fairly standard body shape—any diversion from this brings about variations in the aging rate and in how well aging is tolerated. Here are some helpful generalizations about the aging of various breeds:

Giant breeds such as Saint Bernards, Great Danes, Great Pyrenees, Newfoundlands, and any dog over about ninety pounds generally have a shorter life span than the smaller breeds. How they age depends to a large extent on the care they're given. Optimum diet and environmental management, such as housing, bedding, and parasite control, are very important.

Brachycephalic (short-headed) breeds such as pugs, Boston terriers, boxers, and English bulldogs, tend to age rapidly and don't seem to age well. This is in large part due to the inbred deformity of the face, which causes a problem with breathing. This problem means tissues lack oxygen, a condition that worsens with age. Dogs of this type must drastically reduce their activity later in life.

Injuries Shorten Lives

Working or hunting dogs such as retrievers, setters, hounds, and various breeds of dogs that herd cattle or sheep have average longevity. However, many of their lives are shortened because of injuries they receive while performing their duties. At best they usually have some problems such as arthritis in their later years as a result of the severe stress of their very active early years.

Poodles and terriers usually have above-average life spans if they are properly cared for during their earlier years. The smaller representatives of these breeds are often quite high-strung and active. They need lots of calories but don't have a large capacity for food in their small bodies. Hence, high quality food is important for them.

These dogs also seem prone to dental problems, probably because they get a softer diet than larger dogs. If diet and dental care are maintained at a high level, these little energy bundles can live active lives well into their teens.

Very tiny breeds like the Chihuahua tend to live the longest and age well. This may be partly because they usually live sheltered lives and are protected from danger, although they are perfectly willing to confront a German shepherd if they get the opportunity.

Some people equate one year of the dog's life with seven of a human's. This is an oversimplification. Too many other factors enter into making one dog old while another is still cruising easily through life. As in families of people, some are long-lived, some are not. There are breeders of purebred dogs to whom longevity is a major factor in their choice of what dogs to use in the gene pool. Such choices can lengthen or shorten the lives of dogs of any breed.

It's Not All Genetics

Genetics is only part of the mosaic that makes one dog's life long and comfortable while another's is short and painful. The care given to the mother while she is pregnant gets the newborn pups or kittens off to a flying start or reduces their chances of longevity. Then there are those first few weeks, before you get your puppy or kitten. Are they stressful or is the best possible environment and diet provided? Finally, what care do you provide for your dog or cat? Sound diet, housing that is safe and protected from the elements, visits to a veterinarian when appropriate, and generous, humane treatment all mesh together with the pet's genetic pattern to determine when your pet gets old and how good that old age is.

When Pets Die

Unless we select elephants, turtles, long-living birds or reptiles as pets, the tragedy inherent in all our lives is that our pets won't live as long as we will. In choosing to give our love to a dog or a cat, we set ourselves up to experience the grief that comes when death separates us from a loved family member.

We've heard people say too often, "Oh, I'll never get another puppy (or kitten); it's too hard on me when he dies." A hard lesson of life is that opening oneself to love does bring the threat of loss. Not opening oneself to love brings much more dire threats, such as loneliness and the absence of laughter that a klutzy puppy or a silly kitten brings to life. The risks of loving a pet far outweigh the risks of narrowing one's life. The best antidote to the grief we feel after losing a beloved pet is another puppy or kitten. Not because the new will replace the old, but because life goes on and we do not abandon the habit of loving.

A temptation of this miserable bargain, that pets live so much shorter lives than we do, is to prolong the pet's life beyond what is reasonable for the pet. We'll deal with it in chapter 8. It deserves careful thought.

Before we have to deal with harder matters, let's look at more of the signs our pets give us that the aging process has begun.

Scenarios of Aging

• You've spent years walking with your dog. You notice that although Bozo still perks up when you get out the leash or put on your walking shoes, when you get home, Bozo is pooped and can't wait to take a snooze. It's time to shorten the walks.

• Bounce adores car trips and tears around having a holiday because you've jingled the car keys. But you notice that it takes a try or two for Bounce to leap into the car. You should plan a visit to your vet to see if you can do something to ease the problems Bounce is having with advancing age.

• Tiger has always made futile stabs at diminishing the bird population around your yard. Now you find Tiger blundering more than birding. Age is approaching.

• Racket is the best watchdog you've ever had, but lately people have had to knock on the door or ring the bell before your watchdog says anything. This gets especially touchy if you have people such as small children around who might startle your dog, because a startled dog will sometimes snap. In each case, it's time to find out how well the dog is hearing.

• Snoop has always been keen on hunting, but lately he also seems to be sniffing to find out where you are. Instead of worrying about your hygiene, get Snoop's eyes checked. Judy, a parti-colored cocker, fell down the stairs the first time her family took her to their shore house. She knew her way around the farm so well that no one knew she was nearly blind until she was taken into a strange environment.

Gauging Aging

A thoroughly unscientific gauge of how your pet is aging is how it feels to your hand. Old cats, especially, begin at some point to feel light-boned to your hand. Their shoulder bones feel sharp. Old dogs, too, feel more fragile. There isn't the bulk or the heft there used to be. Everything seems to have less elasticity.

If you find that your pet isn't feeling good to your hand, you should start paying attention to other factors such as whether the pet is eating well, drinking more or less water, sleeping more than normal, or having trouble eliminating. Vets understand the comment, "She doesn't feel good to the hand," but if you are able to follow that up with, "and she's eating only about half of what she normally eats," then you're giving the vet more to go on.

Changes in habits can be signs of age creeping up. If a usually house-clean cat or dog begins messing in the house, it may be that the pet can't wait as long as it used to between trips outdoors. Since this might also be a sign of some urinary tract problem, check with your vet, too. Knowing your pet's habits and being alert to changes is helpful. When you notice early signs, you'll get help early, which gives you a better chance of a good outcome.

Most of us check ourselves out in the bathroom mirror in the morning. Some of us have been taught to examine ourselves for suspicious lumps and bumps. We look at our eyes and we check our teeth and we know whether we're constipated or regular. You don't have to check your pet out every morning, but periodic checks will keep you aware of how your pet is doing. Since you're the only Early Warning System your pet has, it's one of those things you should get used to doing.

Wobble in the rear end is often the first sign that age is catching up to a large dog. The missed beat in your dog's normal tracking pattern is a sign for you to look for other possible signs of age.

These scenarios are signs of normal old age approaching. They tell us that the pet's systems are wearing out. This wearing out, this loss of elasticity and lubrication and tone, is the aging process. As we learn to understand the aging process in our pets, we are better prepared for the same process in our own lives.

Signs of Illness

One point to recognize here: As systems age, they have less tolerance for the stresses of disease. Therefore, our older pets need earlier professional intervention when disease threatens than our younger, more robust pets do.

Some of the signs you will recognize as symptoms of disease include:

1 Vomiting

2 Refusal to eat

3 Restlessness, pacing

4 Unusual salivating

5 Whining, meowing, crying, or panting without good reason

6 Flinching when touched

7 Bloody bowel movements

8 Bloody urine

9 Change in bowel or urinary habits

10 Hunched abdomen

11 Glassy-eyed staring

12 Sudden, copious shedding of hair

These are big, outward signs of inner problems, and an older pet doesn't have as big a margin for error as it once had. It's far better to seek help too early than too late, and the advances in veterinary medicine are so great that many conditions that once were life-threatening now are, if not curable, at least manageable in ways that will give your pet more time that is both happy and comfortable. Don't panic if you see any of these symptoms, but find out what's happening and what can be done for your pet.

A good example of an old, happy pet was that of old Mrs. Sunderhof and her old dachshund, Schnitzel. They lived in the tree-lined suburbs of a large city. The two of them, elderly and dignified, waddled along the sidewalk in perfect rhythm every late afternoon on their daily procession to the corner store. There is no doubt that those two were enjoying a fine old age together.

CHAPTER
2

You, Your Pet, and Your Vet

Throughout this book, we mention that when something happens to your older pet, it's time for you and the pet to go to your veterinarian. The very use of the term "your veterinarian" indicates a close bond between owner and doctor, a bond whose sole aim is the well-being of the pet. For us lucky pet owners, veterinarians throughout our lives become key figures, caring, competent, compassionate people who educate us, keep countless cats and dogs in good health—with our help—and help us through the dark hours if a pet is direly ill.

However, to get to the point of working with such vets, people search diligently for the right veterinarian whenever they get their first pet or move to new parts of the country. Too, they learn to become contributing partners in the care of their pets.

CHOOSING
A VETERINARIAN

When you take on the responsibility of pet ownership, one of the most important relationships to create is with a veterinarian.

Your vet will be the person in charge of directing your pet's health care. This relationship is important all through your pet's life, but it's even more significant during advancing age, as this is a time when more health care is usually needed to maintain the optimum level of health possible for your pet.

You should look for several things in a vet, just as a vet looks for several things in a client. A large part of the choice is based on one's idiosyncratic needs. However, there are broad areas in which people's requirements agree. It is important that these requirements be met on both sides so that all efforts can be directed toward the health care of the pet, not into disagreements between you and your vet. Everyone loses then, especially the pet.

Your Vet's Likes

Look for a veterinarian who likes both animals and people. Nearly all vets like animals, but some have difficulty relating to pet owners. In the latter years of your pet's life, for your own peace of mind you should understand what is going on in your dog or cat, what treatments are planned, and what outcomes to expect. To achieve this understanding, a vet must communicate well with people. Liking people helps in that communication. Any vet who scribbles something on a pad of paper or tells you, "Give your cat three of these and two of those," isn't doing the job, no matter whether the pet recovers or not, because your understanding of what's going on is left out of the equation.

Doctors of every kind sometimes forget that people don't always understand medical terms. If you don't understand something your vet tells you, ask something like, "Can you explain that to me in simpler terms?" The kind of veterinarian you want cares that your pet gets the proper care. Part of that proper care includes your knowing what condition is being treated, what the treatment should accomplish—including any possible side effects—and what signs will indicate that the treatment is working.

However, in this people-pet equation, if a veterinarian has to have a preference, let it be for pets. Your vet doesn't have to be the personality plus award winner to care passionately about the well-being of pets. A vet's bedside manner with the pet is more important than the bedside manner with the pet's owner. Concentrate on how the doctor relates with your pet and put aside any feelings that you somehow deserve the limelight. In a veterinary office, the pet should be top dog (or cat). If we were to rank according to importance, the three beings involved would come out in this order:

1 The pet

2 The vet

3 The owner

The Vet's Ability

Look at a veterinarian's ability to do the job well. This is more difficult to judge than his bedside manner, as often we don't have much experience with the vet before something serious comes up.

Often we choose our own doctors on the advice of friends. This can be a good way to choose a veterinarian, too. If you get your pet from a local breeder, often the breeder will suggest that you use the same veterinarian he or she has been using. Many veterinarians have become expert on certain breeds of dogs or cats because one of their clients raised that breed and sent many puppy or kitten clients their way.

When you're new in an area, take your pet to the veterinarian when everything is going well. This will allow you to make judgments on how well your philosophy of health care matches the vet's, how well the staff treats you, how well the office is maintained, what their policy on emergencies is, and how well the vet communicates with you.

Realize that this is an office call and you'll be charged for a visit. This is money well spent for a couple of reasons. You are having a chance to check out the veterinarian, and the vet is having a chance to look your pet over when it isn't sick, to establish a bench mark on what your dog or cat is like in good health. This can be remarkably helpful when that animal gets ill.

Look at the dogs and cats in the waiting room. Are they all on leash or in pet carriers? If so, you can conclude that the veterinarian has educated these clients about the follies of having pets loose in the waiting room, free to wander at will swapping germs and creating hostilities and fear among other pets. Do the pets look well cared for? Even when they're sick, you can tell a clean, well-brushed animal, an animal that's used to being taken care of. Again, you're probably looking at pets whose owners have been well informed by the veterinarian.

A clean waiting room is important, but a waiting room filled with the latest designer furniture might make you hesitate. The vital working machinery of a veterinary office is behind the scenes, and a veterinarian who is spending money on show may not be spending enough money on the really important equipment or on continuing education.

Interested in Older Pets?

If you're starting with a new veterinarian when your pet is already older, find out whether the vet has an active interest in geriatric medicine. There have been many advances in this area in the past two decades, so you should look diligently for someone who has kept abreast of the field. A veterinarian whose first approach to your older pet is, "Well, you shouldn't expect too much—after all, he (or she) is getting old," is unlikely to be the person you want.

———— EMERGENCIES ————

It's important, especially when you have an older pet, to know how a veterinarian handles emergencies. Of course, every person must have time away from the job. Veterinarians, like everyone else, run the risk of burnout if they don't protect themselves from constant pressure from their work. But if the vet you're considering has no provisions for you to reach him or her outside of normal office hours, look elsewhere for your vet.

In some parts of the country, especially in larger cities, vets refer all emergency calls to emergency veterinary clinics. These are similar to hospital emergency rooms. They are equipped and staffed to treat animal emergencies. They refer the pet back to its regular veterinarian as soon as possible. Such centers have the latest equipment for diagnosing and treating any type of emergency condition, and they have staffs trained to use that equipment and provide critical care for the animal.

In an emergency, being able to get to a clinic may save a life. It may even be preferable to seeing your regular vet because of the state-of-the-art monitoring equipment and the trained and skilled personnel. The trade-off is that you may not get the personalized communication you would get from your own vet, as these people may be busy with other emergencies. However, your vet should be able to explain later what's gone on.

If your pet has a condition that may require care on an emergency basis, have your veterinarian give you a written summary of the care the pet has been receiving, along with what its current medications are. This will greatly aid the emergency personnel in caring for your pet.

In veterinary medicine, we think of an emergency as an accident or an illness that, if not treated very quickly, will result in serious illness or death of an animal. It is important to decide quickly whether you are faced with a true emergency. Sometimes the emergency is very obvious, such as when an animal has been hit by a car and has broken bones. Another animal, also hit by a car, may look unhurt, but it's hemorrhaging internally. The second situation, although it is not obvious, is far more serious.

Guidelines on Emergencies

Here are some guidelines to help you decide what is truly an emergency situation for your pet and what may be only an emergency situation to you as the owner. Realize that these guidelines are not a substitute for professional evaluation. Each symptom must be evaluated in conjunction with other symptoms present, and the individual animal must be considered.

Evaluating medical emergencies, be they for people or pets, is always an art, and is vastly more complicated than evaluating whether your car won't run because X or Y is wrong with it.

For example, loss of appetite is not usually an emergency if your pet is normal in every other way. Someone may have given the pet a handout. However, this loss is significant if the animal is obviously ill, is lethargic, and is vomiting and has diarrhea.

Barring an obvious traumatic accident, any problem that is not improving in twenty-four hours should be evaluated professionally. The older your pet is, the less time you should wait.

Here are some symptoms that warrant immediate attention:

1 Skin

A. Urticaria or hives (rapidly appearing itchy bumps on the skin). Could mean allergy to insect bite or food.

B. Fishhooks in mouth.

C. Porcupine quills.

D. Snake bites.

E. Burns.

F. Foxtails (seed heads of grasses)

G. Lacerations, especially if hemorrhaging for more than five minutes.

2 Musculoskeletal

A. Herniated disc in back. Severe pain or movement injury, or muscle strain.

B. Fractures. History of trauma, won't bear weight on limb, pain on movement, trauma.

C. Trauma to chest or abdomen. Very lethargic, pale gums, cool extremities. Could mean shock or internal bleeding.

3 Nervous system

A. Seizures lasting more than four to five minutes. Convulsive movements of limbs. May or may not lose consciousness. Could mean poison or epilepsy.

4 Urinary system

A. Inability to pass urine. Straining but no urine voided. Could mean urinary stones.

5 Gastrointestinal

A. Large dog retching. Enlargement of abdomen, uneasy, possibly swallowing large amount of air. Could mean gastric torsion/bloat.

B. Severe vomiting and/or diarrhea with blood. Could mean ingestion of irritants or poisons, or viral or bacterial illnesses.

6 Respiratory

A. Difficulty breathing. Head extended; gums and tongue turn blue; reluctant to move. Could mean allergy, or heart failure.

7 Cardiovascular

A. Cough, blue tinge to gums and tongue, weak. Could mean congestive heart failure.

B. Bleeding that doesn't stop in five minutes. Could mean poisons.

Call your veterinarian if you feel there is an emergency. With your information, the veterinarian can decide if immediate care is needed. Sometimes the information the veterinarian gives you over the phone will resolve the situation. Often the emergency is for the owner, not the pet.

A good example of an owner emergency is the case of Nefertiti, the Great Dane who swallowed the head of a rubber kitchen spatula. Her owners panicked and called their vet, who calmly directed them to give her half a cup of hydrogen peroxide mixed with half a cup of water. She would, he said, vomit up the spatula in twenty minutes to half an hour. The treatment worked like a charm; Nefertiti was spared a great deal of discomfort, and her owners were spared anxiety and guilt. That phone call saved everybody a lot of trouble, and no night trip to a veterinary clinic was necessary.

Again, both are equally emergencies, though the owner

emergency often doesn't require an immediate trip to the veterinary clinic.

____ YOUR ROLE WITH VET ____

You've found that special veterinarian whose philosophy and business practices mash well with your expectations. Now what do you do?

Most vets run their business by appointment, unless, of course, there's an emergency. This enables them to treat you and other clients most efficiently. Make your appointment and be on time for it. Few things upset a vet and the staff of the clinic more than to have someone show up late so that the rest of the day must be spent trying to get back on schedule.

When you make your appointment, be concise on the phone when you're speaking with the receptionist. The person who books appointments doesn't need your pet's entire history. Tell what the problem is so the receptionist will have an idea of whether this is a brief, routine visit or a major consultation.

When you see the doctor, be clear and concise in describing the problem. Don't forget any related information. Because our memories aren't what we once hoped they would be, jot down notes before you take your pet to the vet. If you feel that either a urine or fecal sample might be necessary for a diagnosis, take the samples with you. All relevant information helps the vet make an exact diagnosis. Many times the diagnosis is made as the client is leaving the examining room and says as an afterthought, "You don't suppose . . . had anything to do with the problem?"

Make sure your information is accurate. If the vet asks if the pet has diarrhea, don't say "no" if you haven't seen a bowel movement. If you don't know, say so.

Understand the Treatment

It's easy to get rattled when you're worried about your pet. When we're rattled, often we don't think well. Take the time to be sure you understand what the doctor has said about your pet's condition and the course of treatment. The bulk of treatment is done on an out-patient basis, which means that if the treatment is going to work, you must understand it. Write down notes so you can review them at home when you're calmer.

Often we see pet owners leave the examining room and when the front office staff asks what's wrong with the pet, they say, "I don't know."

These people haven't made sensible use of their veterinarian and they won't be of much help in getting their pets well. You're paying for information when you consult any kind of doctor. It's the doctor's responsibility to give that information, and it's your responsibility to get that information.

No Children – Sometimes

Many veterinarians won't allow children in the examining rooms. Because the exchange of information about a pet that can't speak for itself is the crux of what occurs in an examining room, the fewer distractions the better. Children care, of course, about how Fluffy or Sport is doing. But some veterinarians have had so many bad experiences with unruly children that they've made the exclusion rule in self-defense and for what they consider the good of pets.

If your child is the primary care-giver for a pet, clarify that when you choose your veterinarian. That child needs to understand what the treatment is going to be.

Since information is such a critical factor in the success of medical treatment, don't send your pet to the veterinarian with someone who hasn't the faintest idea of what's going on.

Most veterinarians rely on pet owners to report the condition of their pets following treatment. If things aren't going well, you must let the doctor know that so different treatments can be tried. If you don't report, the doctor will assume everything's fine.

If your pet is showing signs of illness at 10 in the morning, don't wait until 10 at night to tell the veterinarian. Emergencies should be just that—situations like gastric torsion or a broken leg or poisoning that blow up in your face. Calling any veterinarian out in the middle of the night for a condition that should have been handled during business hours is thoughtless in the extreme.

Furthermore, it's like the boy who cried "wolf." You gain a reputation as a person who can't be trusted. One of your responsibilities as a pet owner is to be a reputable reporter of your pet's condition, not an alarmist. But as much as vets hate to be called out for false alarms, they certainly don't want animals under their care to die because the owners were afraid to call in the middle of the night on real emergencies. Part of the fine relationship that can build between a veterinarian and a pet owner is the ability to work effectively together during crises, whenever they may occur.

Control Your Pet

On the door of almost every veterinary clinic is the sign, "Pets must be on leash or in carriers." There are sound reasons for this sign, but many owners don't heed the rule.

Pets generally are taken to the doctor because they're sick. Veterinary staffs scrupulously clean and disinfect every surface of the clinic to keep infection and contagion to a minimum. But when clients open the door into a veterinary waiting room and let their dog bound in unrestrained by leash or obedience training, they're jeopardizing every other pet in that waiting room and making their dog vulnerable to every germ that every pet present may be carrying.

It's a sad and infuriating sight to watch a sick, old cat crouch in terror in its carrying case while some huge monster of a dog threatens it while the dog's owner stands by doing nothing. Pets should be tightly restrained in the waiting room. Sniffing noses and visiting should be forbidden. "Oh, isn't that cute—he likes her" is a statement that doesn't belong in a waiting room as some thoughtless owner beams while his or her dog nuzzles your leashed pet. You have every right, and, indeed, the responsibility to say, "Get your dog under control."

If you can assist the veterinarian in the examining room, say so. But don't be proud. If you're upset because you're worried, or if you're not the family member to whom that pet responds best, be honest and tell the doctor, "I'm not the best one to hold Ginger

under these circumstances." If your pet tends to be hostile, be honest about that, too. The practice of veterinary medicine should not be a test of the bravery of the doctor. Part of building a good working relationship with your vet is being honest about how your pet responds to examination and how good an assistant you can be. Some people want to be with their pets all the way. Others can't participate beyond holding their pets for routine shots. Neither one is "right" or "better."

Information Needed

When you visit a veterinarian for the first time with a pet more than seven years old, the vet will want information from you.

Having it available will greatly facilitate getting your pet treated. Here's a checklist:

1 The animal's state of health.

2 A list of any serious illnesses your pet has had, and about how old the pet was at the time.

3 Any current illness, even a minor one.

4 Any medication your pet is on. Take the bottles along so exact drugs and dosages can be noted.

5 Your pet's diet.

6 Your pet's environment. Is it a house pet? Confined to a fenced yard? In a kennel? An indoor/outdoor cat?

7 Your pet's activity level.

8 Any idiosyncrasies? Bites small children? Bites vets? Chews rocks? Loves cauliflower? Anything you are aware of could give that slight edge of information that helps in successful treatment.

This information, plus a physical exam and indicated lab tests, should give your vet a good idea of the state of health of your pet and help to predict future problems.

When Your Pet Is Ill

If your plus-seven animal is ill when you go to the veterinarian's office, the emphasis will be different. All the preceding information is needed if you haven't been in before, but the focus will be on your observations of changes relating to your pet's illness. Important items that will be covered include:

1 When did the problem begin?

2 Is it getting better or worse?

3 Exactly what's going on that brought you to the vet? List the symptoms in the order in which they appeared.

4 Is there coughing, vomiting, diarrhea, constipation, change in urinary habits, change in food or water consumption?

5 Your opinion of what caused the problem.

This information, plus a physical exam plus lab work, should give the information your vet needs to diagnose and treat your animal.

Paying Your Bill

Most veterinary offices have a sign at the front desk that says "It is customary to pay for veterinary services at the time they are given." It can be unsettling in the extreme to take an aging pet in for what you thought was a simple illness only to discover that it's something really serious—and expensive. If a major operation is necessary and you can't pay the entire amount immediately, you should discuss payment plans with the vet and come to an agreement both of you can live with. It is the rare veterinarian who will refuse emergency treatment to a pet because payment won't be made in full immediately. But unlike our insurance-covered personal health care, our pets' care is out of pocket.

Ideally, you and your veterinarian will work effectively and amicably together throughout the life of your pet, partners dedicated to the best quality of life possible for that pet. Without both of you, your pet's odds for the best possible life are lessened.

CHAPTER
3

Health Problems

Because of the changes in old pets' systems, many illnesses that the robust younger pet could breeze through become matters for quick attention for the older pet.

The following is an overview of how each body system works normally, what the most common problems are with each system, some of the signs that will alert you to seek professional help, and what some of the outcomes may be.

This book isn't a medical textbook. We're not suggesting that we're going to arm you with a handy-dandy, do-it-yourself guide to medical care. As we've noted, diagnosis is both a science and an art. As pet owners, we can learn to become informed observers of fairly large, external changes in our pets, but we can't expect to be able to replace either a veterinarian's skill or the microscopic evidence that lab tests uncover.

We're going to help you sharpen your observation skills and alert you to what you might be seeing. Any caution we warn of is based on cases such as that of the people who brought in a puppy who had severe pneumonia. The owners insisted that the puppy must have worms because it was coughing, and their canine medical book said that worms caused coughing. It was very difficult to persuade them that other conditions besides worm infestation also cause coughing. Most fortunately they'd taken their puppy to the vet. Had they simply bought over-the-counter worm medication and dosed the puppy based on their misdiagnosis, they would have had a dead puppy.

Most of the time, if you are alert to changes in your pet's behavior and prompt in seeking help, the outcome will be greater comfort for your pet, if not total cure. If you have an aging pet, you're probably a good judge of what's normal behavior, because you've spent years getting to know your animal friend. This is not a time for you to lose confidence in your own powers of observation or to panic. What all of us need most as our pets age is increased awareness of what to expect and what to be wary of. That's what this chapter will give you.

Two Categories of Problems

Health problems in aging dogs and cats can be divided into two categories, those stemming from normal wear and tear and those caused by a disease. We will address both with the aim of recognizing the problem and then with suggestions for what may be done to slow the progress of the degenerating condition.

The lives of our pets can be divided into three segments, a growth phase, a mature phase, and a period characterized by degeneration. The third is the focus of this book. However, in chapter 9, we'll zero in on things one can do in the first phase to reduce the chances of problems in the later years.

As our pets begin the last phase of their lives at about seven years—give or take a few years depending on the individual—they start to lose the ability to handle the stresses of life as effectively as they once could.

For example, a dietary indiscretion such as pilfering some tidbits from the garbage can, which might have caused simple vomiting and diarrhea in a puppy or a kitten, can result in serious pancreatitis (inflammation of the pancreas) in the older animal. This is due to a decreased ability of the body's organs to handle the change in diet.

All organ systems are affected by this aging process, some more than others depending on genetic strength or previous problems. For example, if a cat has had several bouts of urinary problems during its younger years, there is a good chance that its kidneys won't be operating optimally as the animal gets older, and may fail earlier than they would have if there had been no problems.

Another situation can arise from trauma or injury as a young animal. If a bone is fractured near a joint and calcium deposits are laid down during the healing process, these can predispose the animal to arthritis as it gets older.

___ THE DIGESTIVE SYSTEM ___

The digestive system consists of the mouth, teeth, tongue, esophagus (the tube from the mouth to the stomach), stomach, and intestinal tract. The function of this system is to process foods, absorb nutrients, and, through the large intestine, prepare solid wastes for elimination.

Because this is the intake system, even minor problems impact on other systems. If the pet's nutrition isn't getting to the tissues, problems will arise. This seems to be the most abused system in the early and middle years of life.

Signs of Breakdown

Here are changes in your pet that you should be alert to, since they warn of problems in the digestive system:

1 Indigestion. Shown by a finicky appetite, more flatulence, stomach rumbles.

2 Changes in stool. Constipation or diarrhea.

3 Vomiting.

4 Bad breath.

5 Pain when the pet's abdomen is palpated.

6 Tumors and obstructions. (These aren't things you're going to see; big changes in behavior will lead to more extensive diagnosis that might discover these.)

Some of these changes are due to the foods and other materials the digestive system has had to handle. Others are simply part of the aging process. The stomach and intestines lose some of their elasticity, for example. Saliva production decreases due to increased fibrous tissue and atrophy or shrinking of the salivary glands. These together cause a slowing of digestion, and since the food is in the body a longer time, there's an increased chance for it to cause difficulties. It becomes increasingly difficult for the animal to handle sudden changes in diet.

Regular feedings of a high quality food and plenty of fresh water will go a long way toward preventing serious problems in the digestive system.

An often overlooked part of the digestive system is the anal sacs, two small, sac-like structures adjacent to the anus. Normally their contents (which can be horrible smelling) are expressed as the animal defecates. If this doesn't occur, the anal sacs become full, impacted, and even infected. If they aren't emptied manually, the anal sac can rupture, causing a draining tract near the anus which then requires medical or surgical correction. This is a problem rarely seen in cats.

Common Problems

Here are some of the digestive problems:

1 Decreased ability to absorb/metabolize nutrients. This will show itself as a general unthriftiness or failure to flourish, even though your pet may be eating its normal quality and quantity of food.

2 Constipation. This problem is largely correctable by diet.

3 Inflamed or infected anal sacs. If you see your pet licking its rear end or dragging it on the ground, suspect that the anal sacs are causing the problem.

4 Canine bloat/gastric torsion. This is a true emergency condition which occurs mainly in large dogs. The stomach fills with air and then usually rotates, twisting both the esophagus and the small intestine. This results in shock and severe discomfort due to the inability of the gas to escape from the stomach in either direction. Untreated, bloat will result in death in less than an hour.

The cause of bloat has been attributed to many factors, mainly relating to diet and exercise. Ingestion of air is one of the basic triggers. This may be from excessive panting or rapid eating, and exercise may or may not be involved.

Signs of bloat/torsion are usually ineffectual retching, bloating of the abdomen, which sounds hollow when petted, and great uneasiness. This condition progresses rapidly, so if you suspect bloat, don't lose any time in getting professional help. This is one of the true emergencies in veterinary medicine and must be treated as such.

Many methods of dietary control have been tried. Some seem to work for a while, only to fail perhaps a year later. Surgery in which the stomach is tacked to the body wall seems to be the only way to prevent this rotation.

Secondary Problems

1 Infections of the kidneys and heart valves can result from constant swallowing of bacteria over an extended period of time. These can truly be life-endangering conditions.

2 Pancreatitis (inflammation of the pancreas). The pancreas is a gland located near the small intestine. It has two main functions. One is to produce insulin, which is involved in the metabolism of sugar, and the other is to produce digestive enzymes which mainly deal with the digestion of starch and fats.

Pancreatitis is a serious problem seen mainly in dogs, as cats usually use more discretion in their eating habits. If a dog eats a large amount of fat, for example, the demand for enzymes may overwhelm the abilities of the pancreas. This can result in severe inflammation, perhaps infection, and a sick animal with a very painful abdomen. Professional treatment is necessary immediately as this can go into a life-threatening degeneration of the pancreas.

3 Pancreatic insufficiency is a chronic problem in which the pancreas doesn't produce enough enzymes to digest the daily diet. This can produce many symptoms, one of which is an animal that appears to eat well but doesn't thrive or hold weight. Another is stools that are abnormal in color or consistency, often gray and slimy. Veterinary diagnosis uses a simple fecal test. Enzyme supplements can be added to the food to help alleviate this problem.

4 Diabetes mellitus (sugar diabetes) is a condition in which there's too much sugar in the blood. The pancreas is unable to produce enough insulin, which is the hormone that regulates glucose metabolism. Both dogs and cats are subject to this problem. Signs that might make you suspect this problem include increased water consumption, loss of weight, and loss of appetite. Insulin can be given to pets by injection. Although you may at first be reluctant to give your pet injections yourself, when you see how easy and painless it is to do, you'll very likely feel easy about doing it.

This isn't a condition that we usually see for the first time in older pets, but pet owners should realize that an increase in water consumption is justification for an examination.

5 Intestinal parasites—worms—may also plague older animals. This situation varies in different areas of the country. Signs of worm infestation include tapeworm segments in the pet's stool, digestive upsets, diarrhea, weight loss, in spite of a

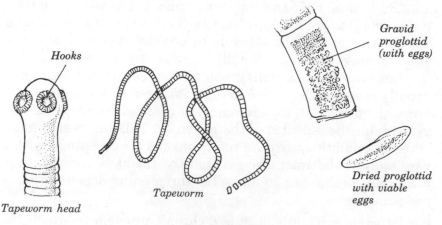

Hooks

Gravid proglottid (with eggs)

Tapeworm

Dried proglottid with viable eggs

Tapeworm head

Tapeworm

good appetite, and flaky, dry coat. Both cats and dogs are vulnerable to such infestations.

6 Blood in the stool usually frightens the pet's owner, but the condition varies in significance from inconsequential if it's a one-time occurrence due to eating some bones to very serious if it's related to ulcers or cancer. It always warrants a call to your veterinarian.

7 The thyroid gland, located in the throat area, regulates the metabolism of animals. It is not as related to digestion as the liver and the pancreas are, but an increase or decrease in thyroid hormones can greatly influence how much body fat our pets have, as well as how energetic they are.

Hyperthyroidism (too much hormone) is common in old cats, such as one with a great appetite who continues to lose weight. The heart rate is also usually very rapid, in some cases approaching 200 beats a minute. This condition can be diagnosed by a blood test, and medication is available to control it.

Hypothyroidism (too little hormone) is more often seen in dogs. Here we see a fat, sluggish dog that seems to be chilly all the time. If a restriction in diet doesn't result in weight loss, we must suspect a thyroid problem. Again, a blood test will indicate this, and medication is available.

8 The liver is related to the digestive system, as well as other systems due to the large number of functions which it performs. One of its main functions is to detoxify the body. As our pets age, the liver gets infiltrated with fat and the blood vessels may have an increase in fibrous tissue, all of which tend to decrease the ability of the liver to function. Therefore, if we continue to place the same load on the liver with drugs and poor foods, while the ability to detoxify decreases, the toxins in the body will increase. The various cells of the body get sick and sluggish and aren't able to function well, resulting in any number of symptoms, depending on the location of the cells.

Keep this general breaking down in mind when feeding, medicating, and using flea products on an aged animal. We should feed the best quality food available, use drugs only as necessary, and make judicious use of flea control products. The liver is a very resilient organ and can handle tremendous insults, but it does have its limits.

Early signs of a breakdown of the liver are picked up through blood tests in your pet's annual exam. A yellow color (jaundice) in the whites of the eyes and sometimes in the mouth and skin of the animal can be seen. The liver doesn't give much obvious early warning. By the time jaundice appears, a pet is in big trouble.

TEETH

Pet dogs' and cats' teeth are probably the most ignored parts of their bodies. You should examine your pet's mouth and teeth at least once a month for signs of discoloration, plaque, tartar (brown deposits that obscure the white enamel in more animals than can be imagined), and redness or swellings of the gums.

An even better plan is to have your veterinarian examine your pet's teeth, clean them, and extract those that are beyond help. The next step is for your vet to give you directions for brushing your dog's or cat's teeth. Many of us have thought that biscuits or bones would do the job of keeping pets' teeth clean, but when you realize that dirty, infected teeth cause many serious, long-term health problems in older pets, it becomes clear that learning to handle pets' dental hygiene in new ways is a major step toward making their aging years healthier ones.

Plaque
Tartar
Gingivitis

**Tooth with tartar
along gum line**

**Normal tooth &
gum tissue**

Your own toothpaste should not be used, as it foams too much and animals don't like the taste. Special products for pets' teeth are available. Most pets will tolerate having their teeth brushed if you start it gradually and persist.

One of the rapidly growing newer areas of veterinary medicine is dentistry. Not only are veterinarians getting advanced training in dentistry, they're performing on animals many of the same procedures, such as crowns and root canals, that our dentists perform on us. Indeed, dog show judges today never know whether the perfect bite they pass judgment on is the result of sound genetics or exemplary orthodontics. Veterinarians specializing in dentistry should be sought out if you or your veterinarian feels that your pet has more severe problems than routine care can handle.

Signs of Breakdown

The signs of breakdown include bad breath, discoloration of the teeth, and problems chewing.

One of the main reasons for dental care all through your pet's life is that it prevents other serious problems.

Common Problems

1 Tartar buildup. Abrades the gum at the base of the tooth. Bacteria in this area are forced into the surrounding tissue as your pet chews its food. This process results in deeper infections of the gums, ultimately resulting in infection of the roots of the teeth, dissolving of the bone that holds the teeth, and loss of the teeth. It's very common for a veterinarian to extract ten or more teeth that are ready to fall out when an animal's teeth have been neglected for many years.

2 Tumors of the mouth and throat.

3 Increase in salivation.

4 Difficulty in swallowing.

___ SKIN, COAT AND NAILS ___

Changes in your pet's skin and hair coat are usually visible early in a chronic degenerative condition. However, they are often missed because the changes are gradual, and as we look at our dog or cat every day, the loss of luster in the hair, for example, escapes our notice.

Most of the changes in aging skin are the result of an increase in the fibers of the blood vessels to the skin.

Signs of Breakdown

1 Loss of skin moisture.

2 Hair drier or greasier than previously.

3 Sebaceous cysts (small lumps on the skin that occasionally discharge a dark material).

4 Papillomas, or warts.

5 Tumors.

6 Graying of hair.

7 Dry, brittle nails.

8 Irregular nail growth; growing around into the foot.

Common Problems

Since it is common for older animals to have warts and various skin tumors, use some judgment in their management. Don't put an old animal through the stress of surgery to remove a tiny wart that isn't a bother. However, the same wart in a location such as under the collar that causes it to be traumatized may well justify removal. As a guide, if you can move a skin tumor, it's less likely to be serious than if it's attached deep down under the skin. Tumors and cysts must be professionally evaluated on an individual basis to determine whether surgery is warranted. Tissues may be submitted to a lab either before or after surgery if malignancy is suspected.

Pay special attention to the nails, as older animals don't wear them down as they did earlier in life, due to a decrease in activity. Therefore, nails may need more frequent trimming. This is easier to do after a bath, as the nails will absorb some moisture and thus be more pliable. If you don't know how to trim your dog's nails (cats don't usually need this), get your veterinarian or groomer to show you how so you can do it frequently at home. If this isn't feasible, regular trips to have it done professionally will be beneficial and improve your dog's ability to get around without the nails catching in rugs or skidding on slick floors.

Polydactyl (many-toed) cats may have one or more nails on their extra toes that curl around and grow into their feet.

Grooming

Dogs will benefit from a bath at least four times a year. Some dogs need weekly bathing for medical treatments. Bear in mind, though, that your aging dog's skin is drying, and unnecessary bathing can make that problem even worse. Bath oils can be used to moisturize the skin if it is dry, and flea control products can be used in the bath. As the animal ages, it will be less able to handle the harsher flea control products, so a more frequent use of milder products is desirable.

Cats, too, benefit from occasional bathing. However, unless there's some medical reason to do so, starting an older cat on a bath routine is going to be a shock to it. You can almost count on confrontation, hassle, and a hostile cat. Many professional groomers who have to bathe hostile cats wear gauntlets.

In bathing your older pet, use a mild animal shampoo. Don't use your own shampoo; animal skin is much different from human and requires special products. There are many available, some medicated, some containing few or no potentially irritating substances, some incorporating flea-control chemicals, and some just plain cleansing shampoos. Much research has been done on these products. When you take advantage of that and of your vet's knowledge of your own pet, you'll have a pet with a healthier skin and coat.

Flea control products are commonly included in the bathing

process. If a regular flea shampoo controls fleas on your pet, you don't need to put more toxic dips on it. Controlling fleas in your pet's environment will also go far to decrease the amount of harsh toxin you have to use on your pet's skin and coat.

One note of caution: Be sure that your older pet doesn't get chilled after a bath.

Brushing

Brushing should be done more frequently and probably is even more important than bathing. It not only improves the skin tone and hair quality, it also gives the pet—dog or cat—pleasure. It's mandatory that long-haired pets such as Persian or Himalayan cats and dogs like Yorkies, Lhasa apsos, spaniels, and all the other heavily coated breeds be brushed at least three times a week to prevent matting. On many occasions we have seen the whole hair coat come off as one large pad of hair when clipping a badly matted animal.

Such matting is especially dangerous in areas where animals get grass and weed seeds in their coats. These can burrow into the skin under a mat and be very difficult to spot, causing tremendous problems when the seeds start to migrate through the body. Cats get mats under their armpits and under their flanks. Such mats make walking difficult and are home to fleas.

Many kinds of brushes are on the market. Some are just fads and others are most effective. It's worth a trip to a professional groomer to get advice on which brushes are best for your pet. You'll generally find them more than happy to help you, for they know what a big difference proper brushing makes in the well-being of pets. And, for their own benefit, they'd rather teach you how to brush your pet properly than have to strip huge mats off a pet that's badly cared for.

Another grooming device that will save your aging pet from overuse of harsh flea products is the flea comb. Cats, especially, like having their fleas combed out, and flea-combing sessions give your older pet a special time of basking in your attention.

Clipping

Clipping your pet depends on what kind you have, of course. On some breeds, certain kinds of clipping seem to be necessary, while on others, clipping is for cosmetic purposes. Many heavily coated dogs benefit from having their hair thinned or stripped for the summer. Consult a professional on this instead of doing what one couple did to their Saint Bernard one summer. They shaved the poor dog, and he was so embarrassed at himself that he refused to come out of the cellar for a week.

Common Problems

Dips or external parasite control products are often too harsh. You'll know this is your pet's problem if the pet salivates a lot after the product has been applied, or if it goes off its feed, or seems logy and uncomfortable. Lighten up.

Quicking nails is getting too close and hitting the blood vessel that's in the nail. Learn to err on the side of caution, as quicking hurts your pet a lot.

Overall, more problems arise from not grooming a pet adequately than do from grooming. Just as we feel good after a bath, shampoo, and pedicure, so do our pets. Not only is proper grooming good for the pet's health, it helps the socializing process and provides an excellent opportunity for a thorough "once over" to check for problems that may be arising.

THE CARDIOVASCULAR SYSTEM

The cardiovascular system consists of the heart and the blood vessels. A healthy system is vital to a happy old age in our dogs and cats. The basic function of this system is to deliver oxygen and nutrients to every tissue of the body and to carry wastes away from those tissues. Reasonable exercise and good diet are

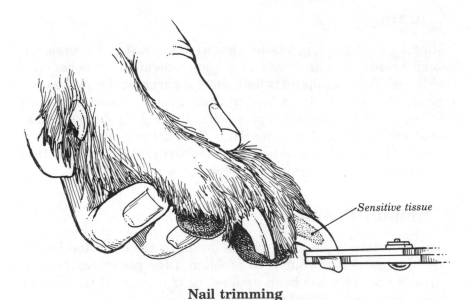

Nail trimming

probably most effective in maintaining the heart and blood
vessels.

Signs of Breakdown

1 Exercise intolerance. Your pet won't or can't walk as far,
run as fast, or hunt as long as formerly.

2 Consistent coughing or wheezing. This occurs if exercise is
forced.

Exercise has to be individually regulated, and common sense
must be used, especially in jogging with your dog. Many owners
who can happily run five or six miles without stopping (although
they may appear to be in great distress to the casual observer)
wonder why they have to drag their twelve-year-old cocker the
last mile or so. The poor dog is exhausted. Use judgment. A
human in good shape can easily run down an older dog. Stops for
water and a rest break are needed to prevent heatstroke in your
dog on a warm day. Remember, too, that you choose your running shoes carefully for pounding along that hot, hard pave-
ment, but your poor dog is running along on the only pads it

has—and bare ones at that. Bloody pads are no joy for any dog at any age.

Common Problems

1 Congestive heart failure is seen in older dogs. In this condition the heart doesn't pump the blood efficiently, and fluid accumulates in the lungs. This results in exercise intolerance and persistent coughing. Many of these cases stem from heart murmurs brought on by poor dental care. A heart murmur simply means the heart valves don't shut tightly anymore, and some of the blood leaks backward through the valve, resulting in a swishing sound that can be heard with a stethoscope. As long as no symptoms are produced, conservative treatments such as reducing salt in the diet may be all that are necessary.

Many things can be done to help your pet with a heart condition. These include diet, medicines, and exercise modification. The best results are achieved when the condition is detected early.

2 Heartworms are a problem in a large portion of the country. Your veterinarian can tell you if these are a problem in your

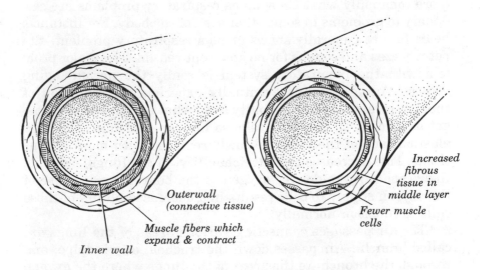

Outerwall
(connective tissue)

Muscle fibers which
expand & contract

Inner wall

Increased
fibrous
tissue in
middle layer

Fewer muscle
cells

Normal blood vessel   **Old blood vessel**

area. Heartworms are large worms that live in the dog's heart and can cause heart failure by filling up the heart and not allowing the valves to close properly. The worm is transmitted by mosquitoes and its presence is diagnosed usually with a simple blood test. Prevention (which is available as a monthly tablet) is much preferred to treatment, which can be hard on an older animal.

Cats rarely have primary heart disease. Some nutrient deficiencies, such as taurine, an amino acid, have caused problems in the past, but most manufacturers of cat food now make certain all necessary nutrients are present.

THE RESPIRATORY
SYSTEM

The respiratory system consists of the nose, sinuses, trachea (or windpipe), and the lungs. This system delivers oxygen throughout the body and expels carbon dioxide.

Older animals have a few primary respiratory problems, but more commonly what show up as respiratory problems are secondary to problems in some other area of the body. For instance, heart failure generally shows up as a respiratory problem—the pet wheezes and coughs for no apparent reason. The major problem with the respiratory system is really the normal aging process. Aging animals eventually experience a reduction of their respiratory system's ability to do what it's supposed to do— get oxygen to all the body cells so life can continue. The once elastic tissue of the lungs is slowly replaced with more fibrous tissue. This decreases the "stretchability" of the lungs, reducing their capability to deliver oxygen to the body. Any decrease of the oxygen supply to cells results in a decreased ability of those calls to function normally.

The air passages connecting various areas of the lungs are called bronchi. Air passes down the trachea, or windpipe, and through the bronchi to the areas of the lungs where the oxygen is transferred to the blood to be carried throughout the body.

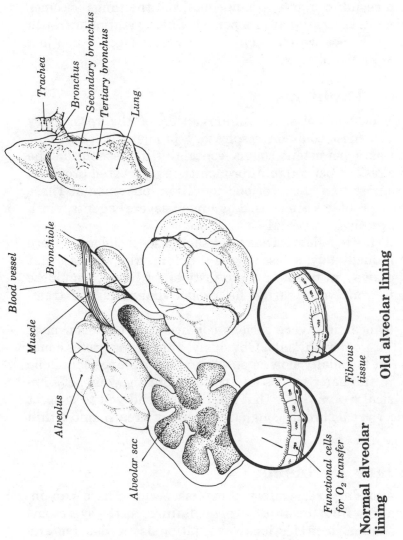

Trachea
Bronchus
Secondary bronchus
Tertiary bronchus
Lung

Blood vessel
Bronchiole
Muscle
Alveolus
Alveolar sac
Functional cells for O₂ transfer

Normal alveolar lining

Old alveolar lining

Fibrous tissue

Lungs

In the old lung many of the functional cells are replaced by connective tissue. Also, there are fewer cilia to move mucous and dirt out of the lung.

Secretions of mucous also accumulate in the bronchi. These are passed upward by small hairs, called cilia, which line the bronchi. As animals age, the cilia begin to lose their effectiveness. As a result, coughing up mucous from the lungs becomes more difficult, especially after a period of being stationary, such as sleeping. Hence we commonly see coughing get worse just after an animal wakes up.

Common Problems

Bronchitis or tracheitis, an inflammation of the respiratory tract, is the most common respiratory problem in pets. This shows up as a persistent cough, especially if pressing on the throat makes the pet cough. If bronchitis isn't treated properly, it can progress to a more serious condition, pneumonia. These respiratory problems are caused by any of several agents, viral, bacterial, or environmental.

A good rule to follow is that a vet should see a sudden, severe problem immediately; a less severe problem, like a cough that doesn't go away in twenty-four to forty-eight hours, should be referred to your veterinarian for proper diagnosis and treatment.

Lung cancer is a very serious condition that is seen most frequently in older animals. Obviously, this needs professional attention. It is usually slow in onset, and its presence should be detected in the early stages on an X-ray during your pet's annual physical exam. Signs that might also lead you to suspect lung cancer are a chronic cough, shortness of breath, and a thin animal.

Secondary Problems

Several secondary respiratory problems occur. These can include anything from tonsillitis to heart failure. As the symptoms may be similar, a professional evaluation is needed for any respiratory problem that doesn't resolve itself quickly.

Cats are well known for coughing up hair balls. The hair ball lodges in the cat's stomach. We've seen cats cough up such enormous balls of hair that one has to wonder how a cat's little stomach could have contained all that hair. Frequent brushing helps get rid of excess hair so the cat can't swallow it. There are petroleum-based products that some cats like that help pass hair balls through the intestines and out of the body. But basically, this isn't a respiratory problem, though it acts like one.

——— THE URINARY SYSTEM ———

The urinary system consists of two kidneys, the ureters (tubes connecting the kidneys to the bladder), the urinary bladder, and the urethra, which is the tube through which the urine passes from the bladder to the outside of the animal's body. This is the cleansing or flushing system. It cleans the blood and excretes the liquid waste.

Signs of Breakdown

As aging occurs, the number and size of the functional units in the kidneys decrease. In time the ability of the kidneys to concentrate urine decreases, resulting in an increased volume of a more dilute urine. Your pet will have to urinate more frequently. But as the kidneys function less and less efficiently, waste products in the body aren't being filtered out as well as they used to be. The net result is a slow buildup of toxins in the body. Sometimes, in serious cases, you may smell urine on your pet's breath. Get your pet to a veterinarian immediately, because poisons are rapidly building up in its body.

This normal aging of the urinary system is another reason to be careful about what goes into our older pets' bodies, because the system that does the cleansing is working at increasingly lower efficiency, so we shouldn't overburden it. The annual check-up will tell us how well our pet's kidneys are functioning through a blood test called a BUN, for Blood Urea Nitrogen.

Common Problems

The kidneys may fail to produce any urine. This is called renal shutdown. Toxins accumulate rapidly, and usually death occurs.

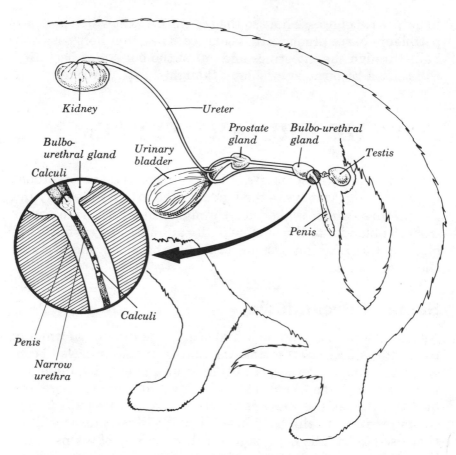

A schematic drawing of the male cat's urinary tract, showing some of the places that urinary calculi may block the flow of urine.

The kidneys and the bladder may be the sites of infections. Changes in the appearance of the urine or the ability to urinate are signs of an infection. You might see bloody urine or your pet might make frequent attempts to urinate or strain after urinating. Any of these signs tell you that a trip to the vet with, if possible, a urine sample, is necessary.

Crystals can form in the urine of cats and dogs, at times producing stones in the bladder. Note that in pets we speak of "bladder stones" instead of "kidney stones." Such stones are due to many factors, but diet and water are the biggest culprits.

The most likely cause of bladder stones in cats is lower quality, inexpensive food. A diet with too much magnesium can produce crystals in the urine. These irritate the bladder, causing an increase in mucous which combines with the crystals to produce a plug in the small urethra of the male cat. This is truly an emergency situation; if help isn't sought immediately, death will occur.

Signs of bladder stones include straining to urinate, blood in the urine, and urinating in odd places (especially true of cats).

THE MUSCULOSKELETAL SYSTEM

For the sake of brevity, we'll refer to this as the M-S system. It's made up of the muscles, bones, joints, ligaments (holding the joints together), and tendons (that hook muscles to bones). Simply put, this system functions to hold our pets together and move them around.

Signs of Breakdown

Some of the most easily observable problems of aging occur in the M-S system. That doesn't mean that these problems don't cause our pets a lot of discomfort. Probably most chronic or long-lasting pain involves this system. Dogs are more vulnerable than cats to chronic M-S problems. Other than loss of muscle tone in older cats, it isn't common to see many problems.

Usually, as pet owners, we're aware of these problems developing. "Old Rex isn't as spry as he used to be" is commonly heard in veterinary offices. This is a sign of normal aging. Occasionally the progress of the breakdown is so slow that it takes a comment from someone who doesn't see the pet often to jar our memory so we realize that our old friend is slowing down.

Problems of the muscles and tendons, including inflammation and soreness, are usually less severe than bone and ligament problems. Too much exercise or straining from exertion can cause soreness and inflammation. Throwing Frisbees for

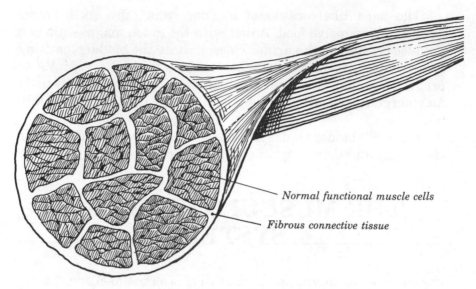

Normal functional muscle cells

Fibrous connective tissue

X-section of normal muscle

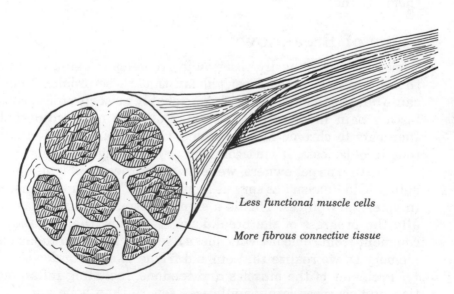

Less functional muscle cells

More fibrous connective tissue

X-section of old muscle

your old dog needs to be restricted. Make the game more gentle so that strenuous leaps aren't necessary. The spirit is still no doubt willing, but the body may not be up to the necessary effort.

The ligaments are fibrous tissues that hold bones together at the joints. They are mostly affected by injury, though occasionally tumors can develop in them. Ligaments tend to lose their tone or tensile strength with normal aging, making a looser joint. This increased laxity can predispose pets to arthritis, which is an inflammation of the joint.

Common Problems

Troubles involving the M-S system vary from mild muscle stiffness and various types of arthritis to cancer of the bones and other tissues. Early bone cancer can resemble rheumatism, so any problem should be diagnosed early in order to start appropriate therapy.

Early diagnosis of diseases of the M-S system is important because these diseases usually come on slowly, and much time is frequently required to resolve the problem. For example, it's much easier to treat and resolve a small calcium deposit around a joint than one that is very large and nearly impossible to remove.

1 Cancer. Whether there is more cancer among pets or whether our diagnostic methods are better than they used to be is a moot question. Veterinarians are seeing more cancer than they used to. Without being alarmists, let us emphasize that early intervention is the course of action most likely to produce what every pet owner hopes for—a good outcome.

2 Tendonitis is an inflammation of the tendons, often caused by strenuous exercise.

3 Arthritis is sometimes seen as a simple inflammation around a single joint. However, many joints can also be involved. Some pets recover with treatment at an early stage, while others go on to develop more severe conditions.

4 Degeneration of joint surfaces is a worst-case arthritis. This is a very painful condition and in its later stages virtually

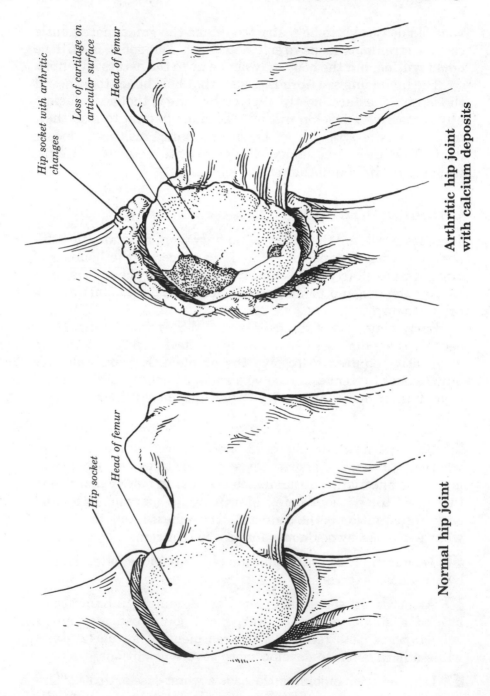

Hip socket with arthritic changes

Loss of cartilage on articular surface

Head of femur

Arthritic hip joint with calcium deposits

Hip socket

Head of femur

Normal hip joint

incurable. All too many of the larger breeds of dogs go through their later years in misery due to hip dysplasia, which is a degeneration of the hip joint. Signs of hip dysplasia range from painful-appearing walking to such incapacitation that the dog has to be helped to its feet before it can walk. We'll discuss this further in chapter 9 when we deal with prevention.

5 Slipped disc is a common problem in older dogs, though almost never in cats. It affects both the nervous system and the M-S system.

The spinal cord of pets runs down the back from the brain to the tail, encased in the vertebrae of the spine (see illustration).

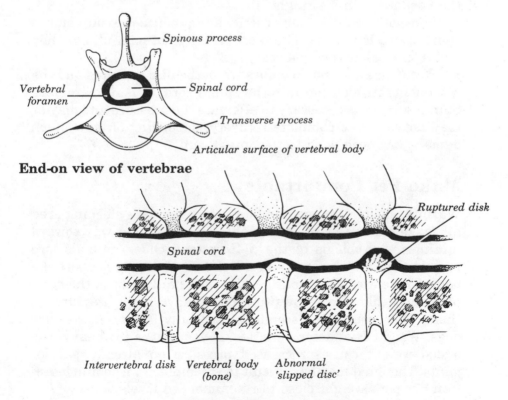

Spinous process

Vertebral foramen

Spinal cord

Transverse process

Articular surface of vertebral body

End-on view of vertebrae

Ruptured disk

Spinal cord

Intervertebral disk   Vertebral body (bone)   Abnormal 'slipped disc'

Side view of back showing stages of disc protrusion

Encased in this bony environment, it's usually well protected from injury, with one exception. Between each vertebra is a little "shock absorber" called an intervertebral disc. These reduce the shock of the bones contacting each other as the animal moves. They are structurally somewhat like a small pillow, with a covering and some internal contents. Due to some biomechanical stress, occasionally one of these discs will protrude up and put pressure on the spinal cord (see illustration). This results in extreme pain when the back moves, often causing the animal to cry out in pain. The muscles go into spasm as the body tries to "splint" itself and reduce further damage. Treatment usually consists of anti-inflammatory medicines and rest so the muscles will relax and allow the disc to reposition itself. At this time, the less the dog moves, the better. If it must be picked up, lift it so the back stays in a straight line.

Some of these discs may calcify and produce pressure on the spine over a long time. These are usually not painful, but they result in weakness of the rear legs.

A worst-case scenario occurs when the disc ruptures and the contents protrude deep into the spinal cord, causing paralysis. Spinal surgery is necessary to alleviate the pressure and may or may not lead to a complete recovery, depending on how much damage has been done to the spinal cord.

Make Pet Comfortable

Warmth, shelter, and padding for your older pet's sleeping area all make old age more comfortable and go a long way toward minimizing problems of the M-S system. Older animals lose muscle tone, which results in a lessened ability to support the body. Therefore, when your pet lies on a hard surface, the bony projections like the elbows and hocks have more pressure on them. This results in discomfort, especially for larger, heavier dogs. Weight is a factor here, too. If your pet is too heavy, the added weight causes increased pressure on already painful joints. Though it may be difficult to accomplish, we should maintain our pet's weight close to recommended levels.

Many therapies are available to treat M-S problems, ranging from providing a softer bed to surgical joint replacement. Many medicines are available, nutrition is important, and some less orthodox methods such as acupuncture, homeopathy, and herbal preparations are quite often effective. But in this system especially, your first line of defense is early diagnosis and treatment to preserve a pain-free life for an aging pet.

THE REPRODUCTIVE
———————— SYSTEM ————————

The reproductive system consists of the ovaries, uterus, and vagina in the female, and the testicles, prostate, and penis of the male. This system is most active in the young, healthy pet. As animals age, their reproductive activities decrease, although this does not necessarily happen without the intervention of surgery.

The bitch or queen will get to a point where putting her through the stress of having a litter is dangerous to her health. Although many pet owners spay their young females in the interest of population control, the owners of valuable purebreds do not. Yet there is a time when spaying may be at least life-extending, if not actually life-saving.

Although neutering is occasionally medically necessary for aging purebred dogs and toms, the aging male is more likely to lose his ability to produce enough sperm to generate living offspring. Surgery, except in cases of medical necessity, is unnecessary to interrupt the breeding cycle, which also isn't generally life-threatening to males.

In America, untold millions of unwanted dogs and cats are killed every year in our animal control and humane society shelters because there are not enough homes for all the puppies and kittens that are produced. We all should use our influence to convince others of the need for responsible pet ownership, especially in the area of reproduction. This applies to male as well as female pets. It seems immoral to allow indiscriminate breeding of our dogs and cats, no matter what personal justification we may invent for doing so, adding to the production of animals for which there are no homes. They are either condemned to death or to a miserable existence as strays, living off garbage and causing problems for themselves and people in their attempts to survive. A few days of volunteer work at the local humane society might convince people to end this national disgrace.

Signs of Breakdown

In normal aging, tissues lose their elasticity. This is as true of the reproductive system as it is of any other system. For the female, this translates to a loss of muscle tone in the uterus. As the uterus becomes less and less elastic, the strong muscle contractions necessary to the birth process aren't possible. Thus, the old female who was bred either through plan or accident is forced into either long, unproductive labor or surgical delivery of the pups or kits.

This loss of muscle tone isn't observable, so even the most valuable breeding female should be taken off the production line sometime around her seventh year, when the aging process is beginning. Having her spayed at a healthy seven years old can be extremely beneficial to her longevity and is far preferable to subjecting her to an emergency Caesarian section when she's a debilitated ten.

Common Problems

The incidence of mammary tumors is much higher in unspayed females than in spayed ones. One or more of the mammary glands become swollen, and the area around them may also be swollen. Hot compresses may reduce the swelling and discomfort, but many of these tumors become malignant, so a tissue sample should be checked. Periodic mammary examinations on your females are necessary so tumors can be diagnosed early.

Urinary incontinence is seen sometimes in spayed bitches. This condition is due to a lack of the hormones which tend to control the sphincter, a muscle around the neck of the bladder that controls urine outflow. Usually the involuntary incontinence occurs during the pet's sleep. The problem is usually corrected either with hormones or more natural methods, depending on the choice of your veterinarian.

Older bitches occasionally show an inflammation of the skin above the vulva. This area can become contaminated with urine, and infection is common. A simple surgical removal of the flap of skin will permanently resolve the problem.

Enlargement of the prostate gland is the most common reproductive health problem with males. If medication does not resolve this, neutering is the next step.

Care of the Older Stud

The aging male often goes on being a productive stud for years after his seventh birthday. Good nutrition is even more important than it was in his younger years. Consider him a working dog and feed him accordingly.

Besides his extra sound diet, the stud may benefit from alternative therapies. There are herbal and homeopathic products that, prescribed by a knowledgeable practitioner, can help extend his stamina. It is usually lack of stamina, not lack of interest or willingness, that halts the aging stud.

Services are available now that collect semen from older dogs and preserve it by freezing. This can extend the reproductive capacity of a dog indefinitely. However, conception rates from artificial insemination in canines may not be as high as in normal breedings. Further, registration of the offspring may be a problem. Deal with this before you go to the trouble and expense of an artificial insemination.

—— THE NERVOUS SYSTEM ——

The nervous system consists of the brain, the spinal cord, and the nerves, which extend from the spinal cord to the extremities of the body. The major function of this system is to animate the muscles, both voluntary and involuntary, throughout the body. You might think of the nervous system as analogous to the electrical system in your car. If it's on the blink, nothing works.

Signs of Breakdown

The signs of breakdown of this system are most commonly signs of wearing out, rather than of disease. These changes tend to be progressive, and most are relatively incurable. If they occur only occasionally, probably treatment is not warranted.

The most common situation involving the brain in older pets is senility. This can manifest itself in many ways. An older dog will get into a corner, then can't figure out how to get out. Another will stare off into space, barking incessantly. Occasionally older cats will not be able to find the way home, even if it's not far. Showing the cat how to get home once or twice seems to solve this problem. Once in a while sedation for an evening will help. Sometimes nothing seems to work. Your veterinarian can advise you.

A major change in bowel and/or urinary habits is another common problem. A once fastidious animal no longer cares to make the effort. More frequent trips outside or extra cat boxes may help. However, it's important to diagnose the cause of incontinence, because it may be an offshoot of senility, and thus stem from the brain, or a sign of spinal cord degeneration. In this second type, the electrical impulse that tells the bowel or bladder to evacuate isn't getting all the way through. Your veterinarian can sometimes suggest things to do about retarding this process. Products such as lecithin or supplements containing choline may help. It's worth a try, as occasionally some improvement, or at least a slowing of the process, can be achieved.

Epileptic-type seizures can occur in old dogs. This is not common unless the animal has had the condition since it was younger. If an aging dog starts having seizures, there are five points to be aware of:

1 Most seizures don't last for more than a minute or two, although thirty seconds can seem like an hour.

2 Seizures are more dramatic than dangerous.

3 Keep the pet from falling and hurting itself. Don't worry that it will "swallow its tongue." Keep your hands out of its mouth, because you can get hurt.

4 After a pet has a seizure, get it checked by a vet.

5 If a seizure lasts more than a minute or two, get professional help fast. It may be the result of poisoning. Seizures also result from hypoglycemia (low blood sugar), a condition that can be treated.

Strokes are not supposed to occur in dogs, but in practice we see a similar condition after dogs get to approximately ten years old. There is usually a sudden onset either of paralysis or going around in circles. Sometimes the animal is only unsteady on its feet. A small stroke can show up only as a sort of brief fugue state, a brief period of time when the pet seems "out of it." Most dogs recover more rapidly and more fully than humans with this problem, so don't put an old pet to sleep because one day there is a problem. Your pet may be off its feed for a day or so, and you may have to feed and water it by hand until it can eat and drink on its own again.

The dog may be disoriented for a few hours to a day or so. Larger dogs often have a wide-legged walk with the rear legs after strokes, as if they're balancing themselves more carefully. Most pets recover well from mild strokes in a week. There are no hard and fast rules here, so get professional advice for your situation. We've seen dogs live for several happy, comfortable, and complete years after strokes.

Spinal cord problems in older animals are usually confined to a gradual degeneration of the spinal cord. This is seen especially in old shepherds and Dobermans. The dog will have difficulty walking. The rear end may sway, or the hind feet are knuckled under with the toes under the feet when the dog walks.

The big difference between this condition and hip dysplasia is that this dog is in no pain unless it also has arthritis. On these dogs, aspirin for two or three days produces absolutely no results, while an arthritic dog treated this way will usually improve somewhat. Spinal cord degeneration has proved to be virtually incurable, and various environmental changes may be necessary.

Small carts are available which support the back legs while the dog propels itself along with the front legs. Most dogs adapt well after a short period of getting used to the contraption rolling along behind them.

This condition may progress to total incontinence. When this occurs, euthanasia may need to be considered. Get a recommendation from your vet, for palliation may be possible.

The peripheral nerves of old animals usually don't present many problems. Sometimes tremors or spasms may occur, but usually they are a symptom of pain in another area. Occasionally a neuritis (inflammation of a nerve) may occur, and the pet will lick and chew on one spot constantly. Licking may lead to an open sore, known as a lick granuloma.

Dogs that give themselves lick granulomas are usually dogs that aren't getting enough human interaction. They have to spend long periods of time alone, for instance. All the nasty-tasting stuff in the world won't stop these dogs from continuing to work on their sore, nor will all the bandages in the world keep it covered. You have to become a canine mind reader and figure out how to keep your dog busy and happy enough to get it to stop.

—— THE SENSORY ORGANS ——

The main sensory organs of dogs and cats are the nose, eyes, and ears. Some of the most profound changes in the aging animal are noted in these areas. Hearing ability decreases, sense of smell weakens, and the eyesight dims with age. These may be gradual or sudden.

The most common and most dramatic is hearing loss. This may start at any time, but it's most common around age ten in dogs. Cats seem fairly free of this problem. The onset of deafness is usually gradual, but occasionally it happens almost overnight. In any case, the result is the same. A dog doesn't hear something and is startled violently when one of its other senses gets a message. This can cause such a fright that the dog may snap, even though it never has before. Try any system of communication such as hand signals or noisemakers to attract the dog's attention.

The most serious threat to your old pet and your own emotions is the automobile. Almost nothing produces such sadness as when an owner backs over an old pet that's usually been around longer than the spouse or the children. Everyone who drives must take a second to look for old Rover under or behind the car before starting out, as even the sound of the motor may not awaken him.

The eyes change with age. You will see a change in the color of the lens somewhere around age eight or nine, a slightly white or gray color when you look into the pupil. This does not affect vision very much until it gets quite pronounced. Cataracts can be removed surgically. Some say that zinc ascorbate drops in the eyes may help reduce the cloudiness. This works only in some cases, but it's certainly worth a try.

Once the animal becomes very sight-impaired, as evidenced by stumbling and bumping into things, you'll have to remove obstacles and sometimes you'll have to help your pet. Chapter 4 deals more with this situation.

The sense of smell may decrease with age. This affects the appetite more than anything else, especially with cats. Here we see the finicky eater in full glory. No matter what type of food is offered, it is rejected as though it were the worst morsel. Warming the food may help, but only for a while. This is a very frustrating situation. Occasionally another pet may offer enough competition to get the old timer to eat so the newcomer can't have the food. Any tricks are fair at this stage.

THE OWNER
___ AS ADVOCATE ___

People who are sick and in the hospital need someone to function as their advocate, to alert the medical staff to the patient's particular needs, fears, and eccentricities and to serve as a go-between in a stressful situation. If people, who can talk and tell what's hurting them, need an advocate, consider what your pet needs. Your keen observation and clear descriptions of what you've noticed amiss with your old pet will be valuable to your veterinarian. Although veterinarians are your pet's major help line and are skillful, professional observers, your years-long knowledge of that particular pet can shed light on some little wrinkle the doctor might not be aware of.

It's wonderful when the same veterinarian knows a pet all through its life. But with our increased mobility, that situation doesn't occur as often as it once did. All too often, the veterinarian, seeing your pet for the first time when it's in dire trouble, has no bench mark for that dog or cat. so your careful observations can be extremely helpful. We've emphasized early intervention. But if you have just moved to a city and your old pet goes into a sudden decline before you've had time to find a veterinarian, your ability to clearly state what seems to be different and wrong is vital.

Sapphire's Story

Sapphire, a black Great Dane, moved to northern California with her owner, and soon quit eating. Flat out quit. Offered every favorite tidbit, she turned down all of them. The owner asked around for recommendations on veterinarians, then consulted three over a period of weeks, while the seven-year-old Dane got down to skin and bones. No one could find anything wrong with her, in spite of doing test after test.

Sapphire's owner kept her going by cooking up a soupy mess high in nutritional value and pouring it down her throat. But she was losing ground, becoming dehydrated, and not caring about anything. In desperation, the owner bought a bottle of people-type vitamins and shoved a couple of them down her throat morning and night. In three days, she was volunteering to slurp up the goop her owner was cooking for her. Within a week, she was eating eagerly. Dehydration and apathy were things of the past.

The owner theorizes that Sapphire was so traumatized by the move that she lost her will to live. Having been seriously abused before she was rescued by her owner, at the time of the move Sapphire had known only one safe, happy home in her life. When they moved, she lost it. But such details aren't things a veterinarian unfamiliar with either dog or person will know, and even when mentioned, they might sound as if the owner, not the pet, is suffering some problems in the head.

Interestingly, Sapphire moved with her owner twice more, and neither time did she go through any decline. But on that first move, it was imperative that her owner push Sapphire hard to make her want to live; otherwise she wouldn't have had another five good years.

Sometimes the patient's advocate has to take an active hand with the patient, too, as with Sapphire. Not all treatments are either pleasant or welcome to the pet, but if they're going to make your pet get better, then you have to insist.

CHAPTER
4

Enhancing the Home Environment

Once we get our puppies over chewing all the furniture and our kittens persuaded not to swing from the curtains, we settle down and enjoy life with our pets. Home seems like a safe place. Everyone knows the rules now.

Often, no modifications to the home are needed as pets grow older. Many dogs and cats curtail their own activities, ignoring the high perches that used to be their favorites when they were agile and active, or avoiding stairs they used to bound up with ease. But, just as you perhaps look for easier ways to do some of your routine tasks, so also you might consider making life easier and safer for your older pet.

Stairs Are Problems

A pet owner came downstairs on a warm spring weekend at her new summer house, ready to go for a swim in the bay. As she went out the door, she heard a soft thump behind her. Checking to see what the noise was, she found her sixteen-year-old cocker, Judy, lying in a heap at the foot of the stairs, dazed. She had fallen down the stairs. Nothing was broken, and soon Judy got up and wandered onto the enclosed porch, where she liked to sleep in the sun.

It wasn't until later in the day that the family noticed that Judy wasn't moving easily around the house the way she did at their familiar country place. Here, she was listening or sniffing before she went carefully from room to room or came to find them, using her nose instead of her eyes. The vet confirmed their growing suspicion—Judy was nearly blind. Because she had lived so many years at the country place, she knew her way around, and so didn't bump into anything or fall down stairs. But the unfamiliar environment at the shore confused her, and she didn't know where it was safe to go.

"If you can keep her in familiar places or make the shore house safe for her," the doctor said, "she'll get along fine. Other than her partial blindness, she's in good health for a dog her age." So they barricaded the stairs at the shore house, making sure Judy couldn't wander upstairs and then hurt herself falling down. They led her around the yard on a leash, letting her sniff out where she was. When they left her in the shore house alone, they closed her on the porch where her bed was and she knew she was safe. Bit by bit, she learned her new home grounds under supervision.

Always a fool for rides in the car, Judy reacted joyfully to weekend trips to the shore house all spring, became confident of her new home during the summer, and enjoyed her last year. How long she'd been blind they had no way of knowing, since she'd coped so well in familiar places. With their help, she coped well in the new place, too. Blindness was not the cause of her death.

Solutions to Stair Problems

Stairs are easy to barricade if you have an old dog that shouldn't try them anymore. Baby gates are useful in helping dogs know what parts of the house are off limits or unsafe. The old-style folding gates are useful because they can be folded out of the way when they aren't needed. However, for very small dogs, the newer baby gates that have screen or mesh are preferable, because little dogs can't scoot through them.

We've never known a cat yet that regarded any kind of gate as anything more than a minor inconvenience to be jumped over or slithered through. But since stairs seldom pose problems for old cats, we don't have to worry about that.

Big dogs may decide on their own that going upstairs isn't safe anymore. With little dogs like the cocker Judy, you can scoop them up under one arm and cart them upstairs to bed at night and back down in the morning. For old Danes, too large to scoop up under an arm, you can fix a folding baby gate at the foot of the stairs and hook it at night so the old dog can't join you during the night.

Outside stairs, too, can be a problem. In single-family houses, you can make a ramp for your dog. Apartments with elevators are no problem. But to what lengths you might go in a home where neither ramp nor elevator is available are for you to decide.

One way to manage a large dog that's unsteady on stairs is to use a sling to help stabilize its rear end. The simplest sling is a large bath towel. Put the towel under the belly, bringing both ends up across the dog's back as handles, and guide the dog with your grasp of the towel. Canvas log carriers work well, as these have handles and are very sturdy.

As long as this kind of arrangement works for you and your dog, who's to care whether you both look funny? However, when we say "works," we should consider how your pet reacts emotionally to the solution. If your pet seems embarrassed and fights every solution you try, you may have to decide whether it is worse than the problem. Quality of life is an issue. If your dog is uneasy with whatever the arrangement is, you may have to consider how much longer the two of you will go on.

High Places as Problems

Cats are notorious lovers of high places. Young cats seem able to endure tumbles endlessly as they learn their limits. But it is painful to watch your old cat fall from perches it used to leap from with ease. There are ways in which you can help.

Decks, windowsills above the ground floor, and high ledges are all places from which an aging cat may need to be barred.

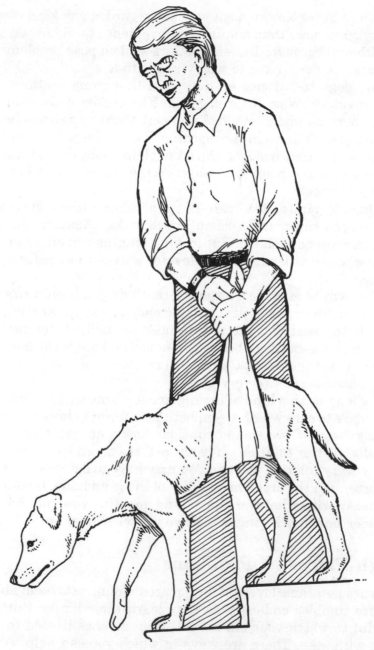

Using a towel as a sling to support a dog with weak hindquarters.

For older dogs it may become important to provide some re-straint so that the dog doesn't fall off a high deck because it can't see well.

Possible Solutions

To discourage your cat from roosting in places where it may fall, use the old mousetrap trick. Set mousetraps along whatever ledge or perch is no longer safe. When the cat lands on them, the mousetraps will go off, startling it. After several nasty sur-prises, a smart cat will abandon the roost for a place that doesn't go "snap." And no, mousetraps won't hurt your cat. They pack remarkably little punch. If your cat is very canny, you may have to hide the mousetraps under some newspaper, an arrangement that also will discourage sudden leaps.

Obviously you can't watch your cat day and night to make sure it doesn't go up where it's no longer safe, and any cat worth its nip knows when you're not paying attention and will sneak into the forbidden place the minute your back is turned. By using the mousetraps, you've taken yourself out of the situation as far as the cat is concerned; now the place itself strikes back.

And no, you don't have to mousetrap all the trees in the neighborhood. We've never yet seen an old cat that didn't give up high branches after a couple of ungraceful spills.

Leashing Cats and Dogs

For outdoor spaces like decks, your older cat can learn to be restrained by a cat harness and leash. Many city cats, especially, are taken outside only if they're safely controlled by a harness and leash, and this kind of restraint will allow an older cat freedom to be outside with you without endangering its life.

Leashing is a good idea, too, for an older dog that might not see the edge of a deck and hence take a nasty tumble.

Another strategy for the older dog in unsafe outdoor places is to sat up an exercise pen. Exercise pens are really playpens for dogs. Most are made of very sturdy wire, usually stainless steel or chromed steel. Many do not have bottoms. Exercise pens can be folded flat when not in use. Once you've taught your dog that

Cat restrained by harness

the exercise pen is where it's going to stay when you say so, you've provided a wonderfully safe place for your dog to be—near you, yet not in any danger of falling or darting into danger it might neither see nor hear.

Slippery Floors

Kittens and puppies and babies seem to take life's tumbles and spills with good humor and minimum pain. But, as life goes on, we all become more wary of falls, less graceful when we take them, more prone to broken bones, and more likely to avoid situations that lead to spills.

Unfortunately, there's a certain chic to highly polished, waxed floors. They're extolled in ads and held up as the epitome of good housekeeping. But some view such floors with alarm, recognizing that a high shine generally means a high chance of skidding. Most dogs, big ones especially, fear floors that look slippery. The bigger the dog, the more certain he is that shiny floors are going to kill him. When you're faced with a slippery-looking floor, your big dog will balk at walking across it. It's heartbreaking to have to drag an old dog across such a space, and generally you should seek some other route.

In a pinch, wet your dog's feet with one of the cola drinks. This makes the dog's pads sticky and gives it more confidence.

Slippery floors are easier for little dogs. They're less worried about their footing, and they can be carried easily. Nor are these floors a problem for cats, who can retain their sure footing pretty much as long as they can still walk.

Possible Compromises

If you like highly polished floors, compromise for your old dog. If the dog is skittish about the floor, put a runner across it on an easy path for your dog to follow. Especially for bigger dogs, an inability to track well with the back legs is the first sign you'll get of impending age. Wobbly reared old dogs can live for several happy years if they don't have to cope with footing that threatens their traction. Modifying your dog's traffic pattern also helps. If one door to the outside involves fewer steps or perhaps better footing, use only the easier access door as your dog gets less steady on its feet.

It's not necessary to set up a barricade to keep a dog off a slippery floor. The dog doesn't want to risk such a floor and will stay off it.

Eat at the Table

You can make life easier for big old dogs that are getting creaky by raising their food dishes off the floor. Some people feed their big dogs on raised tables or platforms. Feeding tables are also useful for dogs that have tumors or other conditions that impair their ability to swallow.

Chief, a Dane who had cancer, was having trouble holding up his rear end on the kitchen floor long enough to eat his meals, so his owner built him a table with a slot in it for his food dish. The table was high enough so that Chief only had to bend his head a little to reach his food, and he was obviously more comfortable eating.

Private Places Are Important

Every pet deserves its own quiet spot for napping. This need becomes more imperative in old age. Especially for the dog that's getting deaf, being able to sleep out of the busy family traffic pattern makes it less likely that the dog will be startled awake and, as we mentioned before, snap.

If you have always kept certain couches reserved for the dogs, you may have to rethink the bed question for your old dog. The couch may be too high for it to clamber up on comfortably. A fine solution to this is to replace the couch with a cot mattress or a covered foam pad on the floor.

Some people keep a stack of mattresses piled in a corner for their dogs. When nap time comes, they strew the mattresses around the room. The best mattress is reserved for the oldest dogs and is closest to the fireplace.

Should wall-to-wall mattresses not match the decor of your newly redecorated living room, shop for the good-looking, comfortable pet beds in many styles. The bigger the dog, the more important a soft bed becomes in the later years, because elbows and hocks hurt if the dog has to sleep on hard surfaces.

Cats seem born with the instinctive knowledge of where the softest, sunniest places for napping are in their homes. As cats get older, they prefer beds with lots of warm, soft bedding so they can keep warm and comfortable. While the older cat seems not to mind an occasional chilling trip outside, it returns quickly to a warm bed.

At age fourteen, Julia Child, a black cat we know, sleeps in until midafternoon, takes a stroll once around the outside of the house, and calls it a day for fresh air and exercise.

Crates as Havens

Better in many respects than the couch is the crate. It's more private and secure for your dog; it's sturdier; you can use all kinds of old washable blankets and mats for bedding, and there's no problem of climbing up or falling out, since the crate bottom is on the floor.

There are all kinds of crates, all on the same principle—a

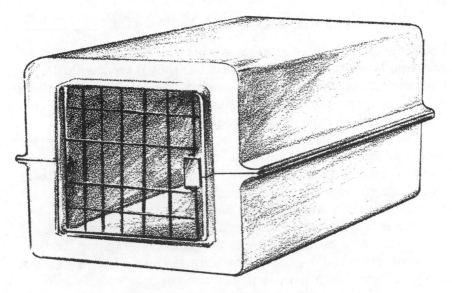

Crate for travel or home use.

more or less enclosed box with a door at one end and plenty of ventilation. Within those guidelines, there are fiberglass, aluminum, and wire crates, and, our favorite, plywood crates with hardware-cloth windows in the door and at one end.

Show dogs spend a lot of time on the road in crates, and dogs that fly must be in crates. The crate at home can become, from the very start, a puppy's safe spot.

Old dogs like their crates if they're placed where the dog can see what's going on without having to be right in the middle of it. You can leave the crate doors open when only adult dogs are in the house, so they can come and go at will. Each dog rearranges the bedding to his or her own taste, and they know they won't be hassled there. Don't use a crate as a prison, where the dog is banished for hours and days on end.

Cats, too, do well with private crates. For a cat, the crate becomes a private nest, and the cozier the better. Though ventilation is important, your cat wants to be able to peer from its crate, unlike your dog, who wants to be able to stare frankly at what's going on. Placement of an old cat's crate is a much more private matter than for your dog's. Since this is a nest, lots of bedding is important, too.

——— AIDS TO COMFORT ———

Lots of pets sleep more as they get older. Though they must be persuaded to get some mild exercise or they'll go downhill very fast, their beds need to be well padded and away from cold and drafts. Old pets are more sensitive to extremes of heat and cold than are pets in their vigorous middle years.

You can spend lots of money and buy well-padded dog or cat beds, and since your pet is old and well trained, it probably won't chew or shred these nice beds the way puppies and kittens would. Or you can visit the nearest second-hand store and stock up on plenty of washable used blankets.

Either way, consider those old bones and make sure they're not resting on a hard, cold floor. The elbows of big dogs become callused when the dogs sleep on hard surfaces. Left untended, these calluses crack, ooze, and can become infected. Two easily available remedies exist for calluses—good old common Vaseline and a dairy farm remedy whose brand name is Bag Balm. Rub the ointment generously onto the calluses at least once a day until they soften. With treatment and time, the calluses will disappear, new hair will grow through the now soft skin, and you'll have made your dog comfortable besides avoiding what might become a serious infection.

Outdoor Shelters

Some heavily coated dogs prefer to spend much of their time outdoors. But even the shaggiest dog needs protection from harsh weather. If a doghouse is your pet's primary shelter, you should be sure of four things:

1 The house is dry and doesn't leak.

2 The floor is raised off the ground so there's a barrier of insulation under your dog.

3 The door or entry is off center so your dog can get out of the wind.

4 The house is large enough for your dog to stand up and stretch out comfortably, yet not so tall that your dog's body must heat more area than is usable.

Pet Doors

For dogs and cats that spend much of their lives inside your home, dog and cat doors are convenient for all concerned—within reason. Cats that are trophy hunters can cause havoc by bringing home live game. Sasquatch the snake-hunter comes immediately to mind. Her owners never did get comfortable about walking into the kitchen and seeing a snake slither under the freezer.

The more time you spend away from home, the more important a dog door becomes, especially as your dog ages. Because most of us keep litter pans for our cats, decreased continence isn't a problem for cats. But many older dogs get so they can't wait as long to go out as they used to. Messing in the house is one of the most common reasons old dogs are killed, often needlessly early. In a single-family home, a dog door that gives your dog access to a fenced yard or pen may be the difference between a good, clean old age and death.

As with beds, so with dog doors: You can spend lots of money for a snazzy, ready-made door that you'll need a carpenter to install even after you've brought the thing home, or you can hire a good carpenter who'll hinge a panel on your door and create a very workable door for your pet. Be sure, of course, that the door swings both ways.

Here's another solution for older dogs. A friend bought a small child's wading pool, one of those rigid plastic things. She put it in her basement and lined it generously with newspapers. When she has to work late, her dog knows that the pool is the place to go. We find that an ingenious solution.

Cleaning Up Errors

If (when?) one of your pets has an accident on your rug, grab the baking soda and use it liberally. It will wick up moisture from the mess and kill the odor. Use a lot. If your dog urinated on the rug, let the first covering of baking soda draw up all the moisture it will, then remove that batch and put down another, and even another. When a covering of baking soda doesn't turn yellow, the job is done.

Club soda works, too, but not as well as baking soda. And there are new odor eliminators that do a superb job, even of eliminating the odor of cat urine.

We're all looking for ways to make our pets' lives happy and comfortable for as long as possible, without having to quit our jobs and devote full time to pet-watching. Whether it's a dog door, a wading pool, or a neighbor kid who'll walk your dog in the afternoon before you can get home, solutions can be found to cope with the aging dog's reduced continence.

Earlier we told you about some medical ways to counter reduced continence. Here we're alerting you to ways to make trips outside less of a burden for you and your dog. Dogs hate to mess in the house. They know they're violating major rules of domesticity, and they feel bad about their messes. If you accept the theory that feeling bad reduces overall wellness, and this theory is gaining credibility all the time, then creating a situation where your dog can continue to be the clean pet it's always been is going to improve both the quantity and the quality of your dog's life.

The occasional older cat that appears to abandon its litter box in favor of all kinds of inappropriate places to relieve itself may be showing signs of senility. After having it checked to make sure it doesn't have any bowel or urinary medical problems, put it in its cat box to remind it of where to go.

Many older cats also become severe critics of cat boxes, so frequent cleaning is necessary. Try changing brands of cat litter, as older cats sometimes develop odd tastes about what kind of litter they prefer. (And mousetrap its favorite inappropriate replacements for the litter box.)

VACATIONS, CARS, ——— AND KENNELS ———

Once upon a time DJ, a nine-year-old Dane, traveled many hundreds of miles to a specialty show because his owners were proud of the old veteran and wanted to give him a trot around the show ring that he loved so much. It was August, but their van had excellent air conditioning, so they weren't worried about any of the three dogs getting overheated.

On the first leg of the journey home, the temperature climbed into the low 100s, and the road beneath the van was sizzling, passing its heat right through the car floor. DJ was hot in his crate, so while one person drove, the other got DJ out of the crate and right under the air conditioner. He was still too hot, so she took some of the towels they always traveled with, slopped them with water that they also always carried for dogs, and put them, sopping wet, over DJ, changing them as they became hot from his body.

They headed as fast as they could for their stopping place for the night, where they knew there would be grass and shade. They set up the portable exercise pens under trees and got the dogs comfortable with no further problems, relieved to have avoided heat prostration for DJ.

They also vowed that there would be no more summer road trips for their old Dane. Their two younger dogs had been hot on this trip, but they never were in jeopardy. More resilient and less prone to stress, they'd been comfortable in their crates as long as the cool air was blowing full blast. But an old dog doesn't have the margin for error he once had. It becomes vital that we all consider the possibilities of a trip carefully when we're thinking of including an old dog. If there might be extremes of heat or cold, it's kinder and wiser to leave the oldster either at home or in a kennel.

Using a Kennel

Lots of people hesitate to put old dogs or cats in a kennel, and that's understandable but not necessary if you find a good kennel. Next to a good vet, a good kennel is one of the things serious pet owners value most. There are several signs of one:

1 You're allowed to visit all of the premises.

2 You're encouraged to bring your pet's bed and a favorite toy.

3 The staff will offer special diets if necessary.

4 It will give medication if your pet is taking a prescription.

5 It will keep your pets safe and clean.

6 It will contact your vet if the need arises and even take your pet to the doctor if it seems necessary.

7 It won't accept a pet that isn't current on its shots.

8 It won't accept pets with contagious diseases.

9 It segregates cats and dogs.

10 Plenty of exercise space is provided.

The people who run good kennels have devoted their lives to caring for other people's pets, and they've learned how to do it well. They recognize signs of illness. In return, all they'll ask is that you keep your appointments on time and not expect them to get out of bed late on Sunday night to check out your pets because you got home earlier—or later—than you expected.

Pet Sitters

Pet-sitting services are springing up around the country. These will come to your home while you're away and feed and exercise your pet. Some of them are good; others are well-intentioned. Many are bonded.

Before using such a service, check references. Be aware that your pet won't act the same way, even at home, as it does when you're there, and if the pet-sitter is inexperienced, problems may arise. The worst problem is that your pet will sneak away and you'll come home to a tearful sitter and a missing pet. Unless you have an escape-proof yard or pen for your dog, a good kennel is better than the risk of a lost dog.

Often a friend or a neighbor will offer to look after your pets while you're away. This can be risky. Are you prepared to lose both your pet and a friendship? It's happened, and basically through no one's fault except the owner who didn't want to kennel the pet.

Nearly all cats adapt well to boarding kennels, even for several weeks. Most dogs eventually settle in at a kennel, but very elderly or nervous dogs may begin to feel anxious and abandoned after a few days. A visit from a friend or neighbor who knows the dog well may be reassuring.

Cars and Heat

Even short trips are more stressful for an older dog. In hot weather, plan trips to town either early, before the heat is up, or late, when it's cool. Even for short runs, pets ought to stay home if it's too hot.

A parked car is a killer in heat, no matter that you roll the windows down a crack. This is true for pets of all ages. More and more cities and towns are passing ordinances that allow police personnel to break into cars where pets are in trouble from heat.

Summer Outings

Heat is a factor when you're thinking about taking your dog on an outing to the water. Visits to ocean beaches, with the burning sun, are seldom the treat in summer for your dog that they are for you. If you're going for a brief time, and if your dog likes to swim, and if after the swim you're not going to let your older dog get chilled, then the trip is on.

Rivers and lakes provide more shade, so the heat problem in summer isn't as great. However, the stamina problem for older dogs still exists. The dog who once could love a day at the river, swimming, sunning, hiking, and chasing sticks now may benefit from a drastically curtailed outing.

Some breeds of dogs don't do well in heat at any age. One summer at a major dog show, the heat was in the low 100s. The judge was checking her books on the next dogs she'd be going over. She was also casting careful glances at the dozen or so English bulldogs clustered under the large umbrellas at ringside, for these were her next breed to judge.

"Everyone's going to want me to put on a good show for them and run these poor English bulls around the ring a few times," she muttered to her ring clerk. "And if I do that, half of those poor dogs will keel over in this heat. I can see them perfectly well right where they are, in the shade. So I'll just dawdle with my paperwork a little longer, get a good look at the dogs, and then keep them out here in the sun as short a time as possible."

That was a judge who cared about dogs.

Old Pets and Children

When a child and a pet grow up together, the pet will be aging before the child is even aware of what aging means. Often, the child arrives in the family when the pet is already an adult, so the problem of older pet and exuberant small child arises. This situation gives adults an excellent opportunity to begin teaching a child about the rights and needs of others. Too often we have seen older pets put to death because they have bitten or clawed a child who should have been restrained by the adults responsible for it.

Our older pets need their own places and their quiet time. Children must be taught that the crate or the basket is the pet's own place, not to be invaded. They must and can learn not to pounce on the pet when it is sleeping. They need to learn how to be gentle with the aging pet. In so doing, children will learn to become more caring, sensitive people.

How much to tell each child about every process that is going on with a pet is an individual matter. Every family handles these life events in its own way. However, one experience of friends shows what happens when you sugarcoat the truth.

Little Bobby had a pet rabbit that sickened and died. A day or so after the rabbit's death, Bobby asked his mother what would happen to his rabbit.

"Your bunny has gone to heaven," she told Bobby.

He stood for a moment, looking at her in amazement, then said, "No, he hasn't, Mommy. Daddy put him on the burn pile. I saw him."

So whatever you decide, stay as close to the truth as possible.

Protection from Attack

Many pets have more spunk than sense. The cat that chases off dogs from its yard, the tiny dog that threatens giants ten times its size, or the guard dog that's always kept its yard free from interlopers are all sources of pride and good stories for their owners.

But age creepeth apace, and even the most mighty warrior slows down. We need to make sure our older pets are protected from their own territorial or hostile instincts.

The healing process is slower in old age, and so are all the reflexes. Thus you need at some time to curb your pet's freedom if it's been in the habit of taking on all comers. Your old fighting cat may have to go outside only under your supervision, and your old dog that kept all strays out of the yard needs the protection of a fenced yard so fights are a thing of the past.

We believe pets should be kept in an environment that minimizes fighting. There is no good reason to have pets whose lives are one trip after another to the veterinarian to be sewed up, patched up, and shot up with antibiotics to control infections that are the result of wounds. Nor is there any excuse to have pets that terrorize the neighborhood, attacking everything in sight. There are also laws that hold owners responsible if their pets destroy others' animals.

The old dog that has been tied in the back yard probably ought to be provided with a fenced pen now. No longer the young gunslinger, that old dog at the end of a chain is still vulnerable to any passing animal or person who wants to attack. Secure behind the fence of a pen and with a tight house to go into, the dog can avoid attack and injury.

The old tomcat that's lived through years of battle needs to be retired, too. Although the fighting urge will never fully leave while he's alive, the neutered tom will calm down and go looking for trouble less often. It seems like a worthwhile gift to give the old fellow.

Again, as with the rest of life, we modify, make allowances for the fact that age brings a certain amount of fragility to every living thing. Around some houses, the joke is that the couches are the canine retirement plan. Old dogs don't have to take their turn in the kennels unless they want to in nice weather, and they don't go for as long walks by the river as they did when they were younger. It's not a matter of keeping a constant death watch, by any means. It's just being prudent, creating an environment in which a pet of reduced stamina can live comfortably and successfully.

CHAPTER
5

Nutrition

As veterinary medicine expands its knowledge of how vital nutrition is to our pets' health, many "facts" about nutrition have changed, and some have been discarded. We urge you to make yourself as expert as you can on the new knowledge about nutrition, for the sake of your pet as well as for your own health's sake.

In our discussion of feeding our older pets, we'll cover two food types, commercially available and home-prepared products. Each has its advantages and disadvantages, which we'll mention. However, we will emphasize that a natural diet prepared by a knowledgeable person is the best a pet can eat.

Although nutrition is a science, the feeding of animals is a combination of science and art. It is an art because every animal is different from every other animal, so many hard and fast rules must be thrown out.

Another difficulty is that virtually all scientific work on aging animals has involved subjects in the age group from seven to ten years. When you couple individual variations with changes within the individual as the aging process proceeds, it becomes difficult to set rules about feeding our pets.

A third problem is deciding what constitutes average maintenance as opposed to optimal nutrition for our pets. What is an acceptable level of nutrition for a house pet may not be enough for a guide dog or a dog that is doing work such as herding livestock. A useful general rule for older pets is to feed smaller amounts of higher quality food than you did when the pet was younger, and feed these meals more often. While the pet's youthful digestive system may have been able to handle one big meal a day, the aging system probably can't.

The owner's preference also enters into this discussion. One person may feel that as long as the animal eats the food given it, that's good enough, while another may want the pet to have a sleek, shiny coat or to be in show condition. We're going to generalize, taking into account the variations as they occur. We'll give you tips on things that our experience has shown to work, as well as things that we've found to be negative.

THE BASIC
——— BUILDING BLOCKS ———

Here are the three essential ingredients of pet food:

1 Proteins. The more active the pet, the more protein it needs in its diet. This need decreases as the pet ages. Cats need more protein than dogs do. While the dog can do well on as little as 25 percent of its diet as protein, cats need at least 50 percent. Too little protein for any pet results in the pet's metabolizing its own body proteins for energy. The result is a thin, listless, hungry animal. Too much protein is metabolized by the body into carbohydrates and fat. We often see an older pet that's too fat, which well may be the result of a diet that used to be suitable but isn't any longer.

2 Fats. These are the most concentrated source of calories, or energy. In our day of constant harping on too much fat in the human diet, the pet owner may be misled and confuse human needs with canine or feline needs. While a sedentary older pet may get along fine on as little as 10 percent (for dogs) to 25 percent (for cats) of fats in its diet, consider such factors as temperature and activity level. If your old weimaraner accompanies you on a hunt for ducks in November and is retrieving in icy water, that dog needs increased fat in its diet. Too little fat in a pet's diet often shows up first as dry hair and flaky skin.

3 Carbohydrates. These are the bulk of a pet's diet. As much as 65 percent of an older dog's diet can be carbohydrates if it is a sedentary old pet. However, carbohydrates are the slowest-burning source of energy and cannot replace good, available protein. Some people who give their pets a home-cooked diet try to economize by loading it too heavily with carbohydrates such as breads, cereals, potatoes, or pasta. Their pets lack energy and usually lose weight.

No Fad Diets

While we humans may decide to put ourselves on whatever fad diet is current, this is very unwise to do with our aging pets. Common sense and moderation will give a much better long-term result. It's very demanding, for instance, to create a vegetarian diet that is properly balanced for pets. While the owner may flourish on a vegetarian diet tailored to humans, the pet will suffer on the same diet. Nor do cats and dogs flourish on the same vegetarian diet, as cats need more protein than dogs do.

The basic idea of nutrition is to provide enough nutrients so that when digestion has occurred, enough of each nutrient will be left for absorption and assimilation (use by the body's cells) to provide for all the needs of the individual.

We must offer a diet containing proteins, carbohydrates, fats, vitamins, and minerals, along with micronutrients (needed in small amounts), and water every day for our pets. The diet must also be palatable so the animal will eat it, and digestible so that it can be used by the body. Palatability becomes increasingly important in our aging pets because they begin to lose their sense of smell.

Moderation seems a good course, even if you're dealing with that feline prima donna we mentioned earlier. Individual differ-

FEEDING INSTRUCTIONS

ADULT DOG WEIGHT	AMOUNT TO FEED
Up to 10 lbs.	Up to 1 packet
10–30 lbs.	1–2 packets
30–50 lbs.	2–3 packets
Over 50 lbs.	1 packet for each 15 lbs. of body weight.

GUARANTEED ANALYSIS
Crude Protein . . 18.0% Minimum
Crude Fat . . . . . . 7.0% Minimum
Crude Fiber . . . . 3.0% Maximum
Moisture . . . . . . 36.0% Maximum

Always provide a bowl of fresh water alongside. When switching from another type of food, mix a small amount of this product with your dog's previous food. After about one week this product may be fed exclusively.

Food requirements may vary depending upon breed, age, exercise and envirnment. Pregnant, nursing and hardworking adult dogs may require 2–3 times more food than during maintenance.

This product provides complete and balanced nutrition for all life stages based on NAS-NRC nutritional criteria and testing.

PUPPIES

Puppies—When 4 weeks old, begin feeding this product blended with a little warm water to form a gruel. Gradually reduce amount of liquid until 8 weeks old, then feed this product with water alongside. Feed as much as the puppy will eat. Feed 4 separate meals per day at regular intervals until 3 months then reduce meal frequency by 1 every 3 months. Feed once or twice a day when full grown.

INGREDIENTS: SOYBEAN FLOUR, CORN SYRUP, WATER SUFFICIENT FOR PROCESSING, SOYBEAN GRITS, BEEF, SOYBEAN MEAL, CORN GERM MEAL, WHEAT FLOUR, PROPYLENE GLYCOL, ANIMAL FAT PRESERVED WITH BHA AND CITRIC ACID, BONE PHOSPHATE, CALCIUM SULFATE, SALT, POTASSIUM CHLORIDE, VEGETABLE OIL PRESERVED WITH BHA AND CITRIC ACID, EGGS, PHOSPHORIC ACID, DRIED CHEDDAR CHEESE SOLIDS (CULTURED MILK, SALT, ENZYMES), ARTIFICIAL COLOR, CHOLINE CHLORIDE, POTASSIUM SORBATE (A PRESERVATIVE), MONO-GLYCERIDE, FERROUS SULFATE, ZINC OXIDE, ETHOXYQUIN (A PERSER-VATIVE), VITAMIN E SUPPLEMENT, COPPER OXIDE, D-CALCIUM PAN-THOTHENATE, NIACIN, THIAMINE MONONITRATE (VITAMIN B_1), RIBOFLAVIN SUPPLEMENT, VITAMIN A SUPPLEMENT, POTASSIUM IO-DIDE, PYRIDOXINE HYDROCHLORIDE, BIOTIN, VITAMIN B_{12} SUPPLE-MENT, VITAMIN D_3 SUPPLEMENT.

This label is from a burger-type dog food. Note that it contains preservatives, that the second ingredient, corn syrup, is a sweetener, and that beef, the meat ingredient, is the fifth one listed, which indicates a fairly low percentage. As you check through these ingredients, ask yourself how much of this food the dog can actually metabolize.

ences will demand some unusual strategies, but get professional advice before you feed your pet some fairly exotic diet.

One veterinarian remarked, "My biggest problem with old poodles especially is that their owners won't feed them dog food. They feed the dogs food from their own tables, not balanced for canine digestive systems, and stuff them with sweets and salty treats. Then they bring their dogs in with rotten teeth, grossly overweight, with all kinds of digestive problems, and ask me what to do. I tell them, 'He's a dog. Feed him food that's suitable for a dog.' Not too many of them are willing to take my advice, and the animal suffers."

Problems with Pet Foods

Some commercial foods have so much indigestible fiber that virtually everything that enters the front exits the rear. Several years ago, one commercial kibble had far too much corn in its formula and the corn was processed so little that it sprouted.

While quick-exit products may be all right for a reducing program, they're not desirable if one lives in an apartment and must pick up every pile that Poochy leaves. Furthermore, over a long time, such foods result in poor nutrition and ill health for your pet.

Other diets are so concentrated that they lack the bulk needed for good digestion, and all forms of indigestion may result. Typical of the pet not getting enough bulk in its diet is the old poodle that eats nothing except a liver and carrot stew cooked up by its owner who thinks she's feeding her dog well because she isn't using any commercially prepared foods. Unfortunately, the poor dog gets so little bulk that the owner also has to cram a stool-softening pill down its unwilling little throat so it can move its bowels once or twice a week.

Semi-moist foods (that look like hamburger) have very high levels of sugar, preservatives, and artificial colorings and so may not be suitable for aging pets.

Growth of Pet Food Industry

As the number of pets has increased over the last few decades and as people are taking better care of their pets, the pet food industry has developed into a multi-billion dollar business by providing people with a readily available, convenient diet for their pets. These products are available in grocery stores, pet stores, animal feed stores, veterinary offices, and even by mail order.

Due to changes in our society, most of our pets eat commercially prepared products. They come in various levels of quality and price. Some are available nationwide, while others have limited distribution. Some are extensively advertised; others are less aggressively promoted.

Remember that advertising and promotion lend nothing of nutritional value to the food. Few dogs and cats take much interest in the myriad of TV, radio, and print media ads that we see daily. We must learn to see beyond the colored pictures and fancy colored boxes and cans and learn to pay attention to what is in the food.

The pet food industry is essentially a by-product of the human food industry. It has evolved partly as a way of using products that we would consider unfit for human consumption, either for physical or aesthetic reasons. Included here are lips, ears, and various other parts that are trimmed off during meat processing. Sometimes portions that are condemned for human food are included.

While not dangerous after processing, these products may have a nutritive value that is small. For instance, after being treated chemically, feathers may be included as "hydrolyzed poultry protein by-products."

A very common practice is to process poultry parts into a liquid called a digest and to spray this on an otherwise unpalatable food to increase its palatability. While this may be included on the package label as protein, it is not protein that the pet's body can effectively metabolize, so the food is not as nutritious as the label might lead you to believe.

Many by-products from the milling industry are also used, including wheat middlings, rice polish, and other grain products. It is very difficult to keep the quality high when such huge quantities of grain are processed for pet food. When you add in the fact that pet foods aren't inspected with the zeal that human foods are, you understand why commercially prepared foods must be carefully scrutinized.

And, just as you may come across a bad batch of some food you commonly buy for yourself, so, too, can you get a bad batch of pet food. You should do just what you'd do with your own food—take the unacceptable stuff back to your retailer. You might even write to the manufacturer, since customer complaints are taken seriously in an industry where profit is the name of the game.

Get Fresh Food

Buy your pet food, especially the dry brands, from a retailer who has a fast turnover. The longer the food sits in a warehouse or on store shelves, the more nutritional value it can lose through extremes of heat or cold or through contamination from other sources. Pet foods don't yet have pull dates on them, as many human foods do, and some pet foods include enough artificial preservatives that the stuff will probably outlast all of us and our pets. You want fresh food for your pet just as you want fresh food for yourself.

We're not trying to degrade the pet food industry, for it provides very necessary products for our pets. These are readily available; they are convenient to use and store, and they are relatively consistent in ingredients. This last is especially true of the premium brands, which are the products of choice for older animals. Another plus is that they usually supply nutrients in a balanced amount so that they can be more fully assimilated. A good rule of thumb is to buy the most expensive pet food you can afford, as it is usually the best.

Read the Labels

Even so, don't forget to read the labels, as all premium-priced foods are not of the same quality. Though price is a partial guide, intelligent reading of labels will quickly convince you that not even all premium pet foods are created equal. Our intention is to clarify some of the terms used and things to be aware of when purchasing these products so that you can provide the best quality food for your aging pets. The efficiency with which our old pets digest their food decreases with age, therefore the quality of the food must increase to maintain the healthy pets we desire.

By reading labels on pet foods, you can learn what products are used, and with a bit of knowledge you can make a more informed buying decision. By law, the labels must list all the ingredients in the food, and in their order of quantity, with the first ingredient listed being the one in greatest amount and so on down to the least.

INGREDIENTS: WATER SUF-
FICIENT FOR PROCESSING,
SOYBEAN MEAL, MEAT BY-
PRODUCTS, WHEAT MILL
RUN, CORN, ANIMAL FAT,
FISH BY-PRODUCTS, LIVER,
IODIZED SALT, CARAMEL
COLORING, ONION POWDER,
GARLIC POWDER, MINERALS
AND VITAMINS (VITAMIN A
ACETATE, CHOLINE CHLO-
RIDE, NIACIN, D-ACTIVATED
ANIMAL STEROL [SOURCE OF
VITAMIN D_3], VITAMIN E SUP-
PLEMENT, MAGNESIUM OX-
IDE, MANGANESE SULFATE,
THIAMINE MONONITRATE,
COPPER SULFATE, ZINC OX-
IDE, COBALT CARBONATE,
ETHYLENE DIAMINE DIHY-
DRIODIDE, RIBOFLAVIN SUP-
PLEMENT, VITAMIN B_{12} SUP-
PLEMENT, FOLIC ACID).

GUARANTEED ANALYSIS
CRUDE PROTEIN...MIN. 8.0%
CRUDE FAT ....MIN. 2.0%
CRUDE FIBER.....MAX. 1.5%
MOISTURE.......MAX. 78.0%

Here is the label from a can of cat food. We found the same label on a can of dog food, despite the difference in diet requirements of the two animals. Both foods contain by-products and both are 78 percent water. Too, this one also had the following message: "Meets or exceeds the minimum nutritional levels established by the National Research Council for all stages of a cat's life." This is hardly reassuring. Minimum nutritional levels are those that only keep the pet from suffering from malnutrition.

However, the label doesn't have to give an exact amount or percentage of each ingredient. For instance, a label will say, "Not more than X% fat." This means that there can be much less fat in the food than the maximum listed, yet the unwary purchaser might conclude that the stated maximum was the actual percentage.

The same holds true for minimum amounts. When you're conscientiously trying to keep an older pet on a low-fat diet for reducing purposes, for instance, you need to be aware that although the label says "crude fat, minimum Y%," there may indeed be a lot more fat than the stated minimum.

This holds true for all minimum amounts, and minimum amounts become especially important when you're considering dry foods for cats, since these should be low in ash and magnesium. You need to know exactly how low.

Some ingredients, such as preservatives, may result in a longer shelf life or may appeal to the owner. If you're serious about optimum nutrition for your pet, you don't want some product that's been chemically formulated to sit on a shelf through flood, earthquake, famine, and fire.

Other ingredients may appeal to the owner rather than the animal. These include various artificial colors as well as the fancy shapes such as fishes or bones, which make no difference at all to your pet since they don't contribute to nourishment or palatability.

Experience is increasingly showing that when a pet food containing neither preservatives nor artificial colorings is fed, many health problems such as bad skin or urinary problems may disappear. When a pet isn't sick but also isn't thriving, suspect that its diet isn't working for it. If commercial foods free of these ingredients are available, try one for three months to see what happens.

GUARANTEED ANALYSIS

Crude Protein (Minimum)	21.00%	Crude Fiber (Maximum)	06.50%
Crude Fat (Minimum)	08.00%	Moisture (Maximum)	10.00%

INGREDIENTS

Ground Wheat, Wheat Flour, Beef and Bone Meal, Wheat Bran, Rice Bran, Ground Rice, Poultry Fat, Salt, Vitamin A Acetate, Vitamin D_3 Supplement, Vitamin B_{12} Supplement, Ascorbic Acid (Vitamin C), Pyridoxine Hydrochloride, Riboflavin, Niacin, Thiamine Hydrochloride, Vitamin E Supplement, Calcium Pantothenate, Choline Chloride, Potassium Chloride, Ferrous Sulfate, Zinc Oxide, Cupric Oxide, Manganous Oxide, Cobalt Carbonate, Calcium Iodate, Garlic.

This label is from a wheat-based dry dog food. Note that the food contains no by-products or preservatives. As with most such labels, this one lists the minimum percentages of crude protein and crude fat and the maximum percentages of crude fiber and moisture.

Avoid By-Products

Other ingredients to avoid are listed on the labels as various types of by-products. These include meat by-products, poultry by-products, fish by-products, poultry by-product meal, glandular meal, and poultry digest. None of these is equal in nourishment to its original source, no matter what type of processing it undergoes. It is far better to pay a bit extra for a more natural product which leaves out these ingredients. This is especially true for the older animal. The liver that once could process and detoxify all the chemicals and other additives may no longer have that ability, and an increase of toxins in the body may result.

Soybeans and Corn

Some research indicates that dogs don't digest soybeans well due to the way they're processed for commercial foods. Neither do they manage well with kibbled corn. According to this research, a kibble based on wheat rather than soybeans or kibbled corn is preferable. If any of the first five ingredients listed on a dog food label is soybeans or kibbled corn, people who subscribe to this theory wouldn't use that food. It is highly possible that gastric torsion and bloat in dogs is at least encouraged, if not actually caused, by foods containing soybeans and/ or kibbled corn. At the same time, we also face the problem that many dogs are allergic to wheat. You begin to see some of the problems facing the nutrition-conscious pet owner.

—— DIETARY SUPPLEMENTS ——

Supplements are a touchy topic. Many veterinarians favor them, and probably just as many oppose their use. However, increasing knowledge is persuading more and more nutritionally minded veterinarians that the pet who eats only a commercially prepared diet may not get vital substances that must be added via nutritional supplements. Remember that what works for one pet doesn't necessarily work for another.

Vitamins

Because no one knows exactly what quantity of vitamins and minerals is in our pet's food, and since we don't know the pet's exact requirements, it seems prudent to supplement the diet. We know that the animal isn't jogging daily or running the Iditarod, so doesn't need massive quantities of supplements. However, the old pet's systems can certainly benefit from a little help in the form of maintenance vitamins. The same maintenance vitamin that you take may be fine for your pet. Consult your veterinarian.

A good source of B vitamins is brewer's yeast—not baking yeast. If you start with a small daily amount, depending on the size of the animal, and increase it over one month up to approximately one tablespoon per twenty-five pounds of weight, no indigestion will result. A too-rapid increase may result in flatulence, or gassiness. Opinions are mixed as to whether brewer's yeast also discourages fleas on dogs. On some it seems to help.

An occasional vitamin A capsule may help to keep the pet's skin and mucous membranes healthy. Once or twice a week should suffice. Vitamins A, D, and E are stored in fatty tissues; too high a dosage results in toxicity. However, new processes are providing A, D, and E vitamins available in water-soluble forms. Be knowledgeable and be careful with these.

Another controversial additive is vitamin C. Many veterinarians consider this "the healing vitamin," useful for puppy sprains, for instance. It's also important in the development of sound tendons. New developments in the use of vitamin C would indicate its efficacy goes beyond what many people might have expected, and it plays an important part in the lifelong health of both dogs and cats. Old pets benefit from a daily supplement of C, since their ability to produce this vitamin may decrease with age. In the wilds, dogs and cats ate a great deal of raw food, including large amounts of greens, which provided them with vitamin C. Since we've changed most of our pets over to a commercial diet lacking in the sources of vitamin C, it seems sensible to make sure they get that important vitamin.

Summing up our advice on vitamins, because optimum dosages of these vitamins depend heavily on your own pet's weight and current state of health, consult seriously with a veterinarian who is sophisticated about vitamin additives before putting your pet on any regimen that adds A, D, or E beyond the amounts contained in a multivitamin capsule.

Minerals

Trace minerals from ancient sea beds probably would help all of us. While little is known in the way of hard evidence about them, it is safe to say that all animals could benefit from them. These products are available in tablet form in health food stores. Look for a product that says "Trace Minerals."

The use of alfalfa tablets to supplement the diet of old dogs that are beginning to have wobbly rear ends is controversial. Over a period of close to twenty years, we have found that for some large dogs, alfalfa tablets have provided the difference between a long old age with a rear end that provides secure tracking and a quick falling apart. Any improvement that will show occurs within thirty days, so this is a home remedy you can feel free to check out for yourself. The dogs for whom alfalfa tablets didn't work had such seriously degenerated hip sockets that nothing would help.

Zinc supplements may help for dogs with flaky skin. Professional advice should be sought before you decide on this one.

Raw Foods

Virtually all the enzymes present in raw foods are destroyed in processing. To counteract this loss, you can improve the nutrient quality of your pet's food by adding raw vegetables. Some pets will eat raw vegetables eagerly. For those that won't, run the vegetables through a food processor. That will make them more palatable—or hide them better in the rest of the food.

Do not feed raw fish such as salmon to dogs, as there may be a rickettsial organism present that, while it's killed in the cooking process, is very toxic to dogs. Also, don't feed cats any fish or shellfish that is suspect. Clams and mussels, for instance, harbor the red tide organism at certain times of the year, and it's every bit as deadly to cats as it is to humans. When there's a

TRACE MINERALS
A Balanced Mineral Supplement
For All Animals
In 1 LB. (16 oz.) powder form

Our unique, naturally-balanced Trace Minerals Supplement asures you that your pet's diet will not be lacking in any of these very important naturally chelated trace minerals.

Trace minerals comes directly from the mine to your pet. There are no preservatives, sugars, artificial colors or flavorings, and no starches.

Calcium	2.2%	Barium	.008%
Phosphorus	1.1%	Bismuth	.014%
Iron	3.5%	Copper	.0075%
Magnesium	.098%	Cobalt	.0018%
Sulphur	2.0%	Chromium	.006%
Potassium	1.56%	Manganese	.015%
Sodium	1.2%	Zinc	.15%
Titanium	.005%	Selenium	.00031%

SOURCE OF NUTRIENTS: Montmorillonite, Plagioclase Feldspar which are known to contain the following: Molybdenum, Tin, Iodine, Fluorine, Vanadium, Nickel, Bromine, Strontium, Cadmium, Silicon, Rubidium, Aluminum, Thulium, Chlorine, Gallium, Zirconium, Tungsten, Uranium, Gold, Germanium, Silver, Antimony, Yttrium, Niobium, Ruthenium, Rhodium, Palladium, Indium, Tellurium, Cesium, Lanthanum, Cerium, Praseodymium, Neodymium, Samarium, Europium, Gadolinium, Terbium, Dysprosium, Holmium, Erbium, Thulium, Ytterbium, Lutetium, Hafnium, Tantalum, Rhenium, Osmium, Iridium, Platinium, Thallium, Beryllium, Scandium.

RESULTS:

Darker, richer, thicker hair coat. Better maintenance of body weight
• Increases utilization of nutrients in diet food
•Improved general health

Completely Natural. Suggested Use: Small pets (40 lbs. or less) 1 teaspoon per day. Large pets (over 40 lbs.) 2 teaspoons per day.

This label is from a package of trace minerals.

shellfish quarantine on the ocean and bays where you usually collect shellfish to eat, obey that quarantine for all family members, including the felines.

Pet owners disagree about how much meat a dog needs. Dogs and, to a lesser extent, cats, are omnivora—that is, they naturally eat both meat and vegetables. Some people mistakenly think that dogs are carnivores, meat-eaters only. Not true. A well-balanced commercial kibble contains enough protein for the average lie-around-the-house old dog. If that old dog is getting finicky about meals, adding meat to its kibble will increase the nose-appeal of that meal. Use canned, raw, or cooked meat, or be generous with pan drippings that don't contain a lot of grease. Remember that you're doing this for nose-appeal as well as nutrition, and don't overdo it. Meat is harder to digest than other foods. Too much meat will give your old dog digestive challenges that it may not be up to. We're talking about old, sedentary dogs now, not hard-working stock animals, racers, or other active dogs.

Canned Foods

Thus far, we've talked mainly about dry foods for dogs and cats. There are hundreds of brands of canned foods, too. For dogs, the biggest lack in these products is bulk. However, they make fine additives to the dry kibble, and dogs like the mixture. Canned food is approximately 70 percent water, so that will help if more moisture in the diet is desired.

Cats seem to thrive better than dogs on a diet mainly of canned food. But check the quantity of magnesium in the food, as too much magnesium contributes to dire urinary problems. Ideally the quantity should be approximately .1 percent.

A combination of a high-quality commercial dry food and an equally good canned food will provide your cat with a highly palatable, nutritious diet. If you have an indoor/outdoor cat, it forages on its own for greens. If, however, yours is strictly an indoor cat, you need to provide greens for it. These may be salad greens, with an occasional treat of that all-time favorite, catnip, which is better for your cat in its fresh state than in the dried.

Keep the catnip plant where your cat can't get to it or you'll have a very turned-on cat for a few hours and a very demolished catnip plant. Before we knew this, we had a ten-year-old cat that was swinging from the curtains and a catnip plant that was nothing but a few little nubbins of stem.

Occasionally a cat, after many bouts of urinary problems, may be unable to eat dry foods. This is rare, and the dry foods are most helpful for most cats, as they are foods the cat can snack on at will.

Home Cooking

Food properly prepared at home is the best food for any pet. However, it requires much more time and effort. There are many sources of recipes for pet foods, some of which are listed in the reference material at the end of this book. These recipes allow very specific monitoring and control of the diet and may be necessary in certain animals that are teetering between health and disease.

If you're preparing your pet's food, remember to include the essential nutrients—proteins, fats, carbohydrates and vitamins. Remember, too, that your pet needs bulk in its diet, so whatever you're preparing, base it on rice, wheat, oats, or barley. Dogs don't seem to do well with soybeans or several kinds of corn. Add to the basic bulk some vegetables and meat. Especially for older animals, the mixture may be rather soupy. Experiment for nose appeal and, of course, general thriftiness. The entire point of home cooking instead of using commercial foods is to improve health.

Many of us compromise, using a high-quality commercial kibble as the base, then stewing up soup bones, vegetables, and maybe rice or barley with which we moisten the dry food. The old-timers slurp it up like hungry puppies.

Brief Dietary Tips

DON'T

• Give your old dog cooked bones. A splintered bone can mean a dead pet.

- Give your dog raw fish, especially salmon. Parasites may be present that can make your dog very sick.

- Leave your pet's canned or moistened food standing in the dish. Spoilage can occur, and your pet will have indigestion at the very least. (Dry food is an excellent snack.)

- Give your dog raw eggs. They destroy an important digestive enzyme in the intestines.

- Change the basic food all the time. Add pan juices or other niceties for nose appeal and variety.

- Encourage your old dog to play roughly after a meal. Digestion is slowed down in old age.

- Put your old pet on fad diets. Get professional advice.

DO

- Give your dog cooked eggs, even one-minute eggs. They are good sources of protein.

- Encourage your pets to eat yogurt. It's good for them.

- Give them dairy products like milk, unless it causes diarrhea.

- Give your pets cheese.

- Carry water from home if you're traveling with your pet. Water changes cause digestive upsets.

- .Make any changes in your old pet's diet gradually.

- Reduce amounts fed as your pet's activity decreases.

- Substitute ice cubes for water if your dog has just had surgery. Better yet, make the ice cubes out of chicken broth.

- Add greens to your pets' diet if you see them eating grass and then throwing it up.

TIMES FOR
—————— SPECIAL DIETS ——————

There are times that call for something special in the pet's food dish. Here are some of them:

• During or after the stress of hospitalization or surgery, a pet requires a higher quality of easily metabolized, carefully balanced food. Such foods include cooked brown rice, cooked poultry, and honey. If your vet doesn't mention this need, ask about it.

• When your pet has anorexia. It's an absence of appetite, as in the case of Sapphire when she moved. Your long-range goal is to restore the pet's appetite, but in the short term, special diets and dietary supplements must be used or the pet will die.

• While taking antibiotics for more than a few days, pets need some dietary augmentation like yogurt, just as people do.

• If your pet has diabetes, good quality food is especially important, along with insulin therapy. Poor quality food complicates the treatment.

• Whenever a pet has diarrhea, it's important to find the cause. If something the pet has been eating is causing the condition, you should stop offering it. If the diarrhea is severe, your vet may prescribe a twelve- to twenty-four-hour fast. Usually the first food you put your pet back on is a liquid diet of high nutritive value. Dry food should be drastically reduced for a few days, as its high fiber content makes the tendency toward diarrhea worse. Bland foods such as cottage cheese, rice, and cooked eggs are good choices.

• After undergoing any kind of exposure, such as being chilled, frightened, exhausted, or starved, the pet should get special dietary consideration. For the first twenty-four hours after the exposure, small, frequent amounts of a highly concentrated source of calories should be fed, along with small amounts of water. Restrict water consumption, as you don't want the pet to vomit. After that initial period, a high-protein, high-energy diet should be fed the pet until it's back to normal.

• Old, inactive pets can easily tend toward obesity, which strains all the body's systems. The pet's caloric intake must be reduced, but this must not be done only by reducing the pet's food amounts. The pet can then become ravenous, and it's possible that dietary deficiencies may occur. There are commercially prepared reducing diets for pets. But think first about whether your pet is given snacks or fed at the dinner table. Try cutting out the snacks first. If that doesn't reduce your pet's weight, ask your veterinarian for a diet.

—————— TREATS ——————

The best balanced diet in the world can be ruined if a pet gets lots of improper treats. But every owner wants to reward pets with treats at one time or another. Here are some possibilities:

• Dry biscuits, especially from the companies that make natural foods, are excellent for cats and dogs.

• Catnip is cat heaven.

• Little pieces of chicken, tuna, or cheese are fine for cats or dogs.

• Liver baked until it's dry in a 200-degree oven is a favorite dog treat.

• All sugary or salty treats are not good for your cats or dogs. Candy and potato chips are o-u-t.

• Avoid commercial treats that are loaded with preservatives.

• Be moderate in any treats. Balance the diet and feed your pet well, and you will take an enormous step toward good health and a long life.

We've included sources for diets and recipes in the resources section at the end of the book. And, to cheer you up, we've had both dogs and cats that have eaten like champions right down to very old ages, happily gobbling up their regular, high-quality diets and asking for no special changes just because they were in the senior category.

CHAPTER
6

Pollution and Poisons

Many of the same environmental factors that threaten people's health also impact on pets' health. Water quality, air pollution, food additives that build up in the system, and toxic products used in homes and yards all merit our attention whether we're considering our own health or our pets'.

The use of chemicals to control the environment continues to grow at a fast pace, and the long-term effect of many of these chemicals is unknown. Although some of the chemical control agents are listed as basically non-toxic, any substance improperly used or given in too large an amount can be toxic.

More and more, people are realizing that where they live is as much a factor in how they feel as disease is. What kind of toxins are the factories around us belching forth? What sort of chemicals are carried in the wind that blows softly in our faces as we go out for our morning walk with our faithful old cat pacing behind us, tail held high? What's been dumped upstream in the river we splash in, enjoying our old dog's joy in fetching sticks from the water? When we think about the general decline in an old body's ability to cope with toxins and stresses it once was able to handle, we realize that our pets are as vulnerable as we are.

Air Quality and the Older Pet

Urban pets breathe the same smog that urban people breathe. The city cat that stays indoors all the time is perhaps better off than the one that climbs fences and fire escapes, though there are poisons inside, too. The city dog that is forced to run or jog with its owner can be at dire risk, especially in its later years. The dog often runs at exhaust-pipe level, getting the full blast of noxious fumes spewed out by cars, trucks, and buses. This is the time to seek out places to run where neither pet nor owner is inhaling the exhaust from cars or the waste that spews from factories.

If you can't find such places, pay attention to smog alerts and make your old dog's outings short, safe walks. When there are warnings for people to stay indoors or to restrict their activity level, heed them for older pets, too. Indoor games of chase-the-ball need to take the place of outdoor exercise during severe smog alerts.

Suburbia is no piece of cake for pets, either. Many toxins are used regularly—and often improperly—on lawns and gardens. Your cat or dog comes in much closer contact than you do with the ground where such products have been applied, and is at greater risk. If you use a gardening or lawn care service, find out what chemicals are being used on your place, and demand that only products safe for your pets be used.

Insecticides

Many insecticides are available for outdoor use, ranging from sprays to rid your yard of bugs while you're having a barbecue to systemics that you feed to plants to make them deadly to bugs.

Although it may be a good idea to spray the yard occasionally to decimate the flea and tick population, make sure your pets don't go out into the yard until the poisons have somewhat dispersed.

Any time you're using herbicides or insecticides in the yard, keep your old pets, especially, away from the area until wind, air, and time have done their job.

Applied Poisons Outdoors

Avid gardeners go to great lengths to get rid of pests, using many products that are dangerous to pets. Snail and slug bait often looks like dry food to cats or dogs. Most manufacturers of snail bait no longer produce the pelleted variety that pets ate regularly and sometimes died from. However, if you use snail bait, keep your pets out of the places where you've put it. Pets are supposed to dislike the poisons people use to get rid of moles and gophers; however, some curious pets haven't read the labels announcing that "fact."

Most cats won't eat rodents that have been poisoned, but if you've been poisoning moles or gophers and your cat or dog begins to have digestive upsets or tremors, take the pet to your veterinarian. Dogs, particularly, which often have indiscreet eating habits, should be watched for signs of poisoning.

Rat poison usually works by tying up vitamin K in the body. The blood fails to clot and the animal dies from hemorrhage from an insignificant wound. Rat poison is sometimes put into a fish base, which is very palatable for pets. These poisons are deadly. Any unexplained bleeding is an emergency.

Puppies and kittens are more likely to be wiped out by their curiosity about what's in containers than older pets are. One definition of an old pet might be "one that's lived long enough not to go foraging among the containers of chemicals in the garage." However, because of our imperfect knowledge of the long-term effects of chemicals, your pet should not be housed in the same area where you store your garden or cleaning supplies.

Antifreeze is deadly to animals for two reasons—they like it, and a small amount wipes out the kidneys very quickly. Be especially careful of how and where you store this. Also, clean up spills or overflows from the car radiator immediately.

Indoor Toxins

Indoors isn't always safer than outdoors. Old houses often still have asbestos insulating pipes. Asbestos was commonly used as insulation in walls and attics, and much of it is still present. Certain kinds of ceilings have high asbestos content, and some old houses have wallboard made of asbestos. We have laws about removing asbestos from public buildings, but in our homes, we're free to keep on breathing in those tiny little asbestos fibers that lance their way into individual cells, causing the cells to try to grow repairs that often turn out to be cancerous.

Removal of asbestos is tricky; a whole new area of expertise is coming into being as people learn how to protect themselves from the damaging fibers and contain the asbestos long enough to get it into airtight packaging.

Poor Air Exchange

As we insulate our houses more and more efficiently, we create environments in which air exchange is less and less efficient. Not only does highly efficient insulation keep everything inside the house, some insulation itself is toxic, due to the formaldehyde in it. The old, drafty house had something positive going for it—at least when one family member had a cold, all the germs didn't stay in the house for everyone else to acquire. Today we hear about "the sick building" syndrome, a condition in which toxins of all kinds are kept inside the building because of poor air exchange. If you consider the myriad of cleaning compounds we use in our homes, if there isn't good air exchange with the outside, we and our pets are breathing a strange and possibly lethal concoction. If you're being energy-responsible and planning to insulate your house, ask penetrating questions about the materials that are being used, making as sure as you can of their non-toxicity. Locate a local environmental group to find out more.

Add to the concoction of normal cleaning compounds some of the preservatives that are used on lumber and some of the chemicals that go into making plywood and you begin to understand why there are many pets and people who are not actively sick, but who are never truly well, either.

If you've just moved to a brand-new house and your old pet is acting sick, consult with your veterinarian about what might be the cause. You may have to create better air exchange and circulation. In extreme cases, you may have to get your contractor to mitigate some of the toxins. Certainly if you use a janitorial service, you need to make sure the personnel isn't using chemicals in your house that will adversely affect your old pet.

Cats seem to be even more susceptible than dogs to environmental pollutants in the home. Pay special attention to floor cleaners and keep cats off them until they're dry, as cats may lick these products off their paws. Especially common are cats with liver problems long before one would expect such problems. We can only believe this condition has been caused by an accretion of toxins in the environment.

Rugs

Rugs may be causing indoor problems for you and your pets. Since your pets spend much of their lives lying on your rugs, they get a heavy dose of any toxins there. The potential culprits are chemicals used in the manufacturing process. The best bet for you and your pets is to look for natural fibers that haven't been chemically drenched in the manufacturing process. Pay careful attention to whatever beds you might buy for the comfort of your old pet; go for natural fibers that are less likely to rouse allergies.

Air Conditioning

Air conditioners are major culprits in spreading pollution inside buildings. In many high-rise offices, an outbreak of flu on the fourth floor, for instance, quickly travels via air conditioning systems to the fifth and sixth floors. The same phenomenon may be traced through a high rise apartment building where air exchange is dependent on a filtering system rather than on outside air being introduced into each living unit. Even in single-family homes, the air conditioner can spread molds and spores if it isn't clean or functioning properly.

Radon Gas

One of the invisible poisons in many parts of the country is radon, a gas that seeps up from the ground. Home test kits are available, and, in some places, correction of the problem is relatively easy and inexpensive. Then there is the question of what use was made of the land where your house is now. The lessons of Love Canal should not be forgotten.

All of the poisons that affect people in their homes also affect pets. Much of our medicine, be it human or veterinary, needs to be concerned not only with what seems to be wrong with us, but also with where we live and what toxins are around us there.

Indoor Insecticides

Many people saturate their homes inside with various pesticides. Some of these, like the periodic bombing for fleas and ticks, are necessary for the health of people and pets alike if we live where such parasites flourish. If you follow the directions on such products carefully, paying special attention to the thorough airing the house is supposed to have before either people or pets move back inside, most of these products are beneficial.

Much of the damage caused by home-applied pesticides is done either through improper use of the product, careless storage of opened containers, or improper disposal of the empty containers. A thoughtful inventory of what's stored in the cupboards under most kitchen sinks would make the average pet owner do a thorough cleaning out of that closet of chemical horrors.

Poisons such as ant buttons are open temptations to pets of all ages. The older pet isn't necessarily beyond tasting some interesting smelling stuff that might be a tidbit. Most substances that can kill insects or rodents can at least make a pet sick. If we're talking about a small older pet that's already teetering on the brink between sickness and health, getting into household poison can be a dire experience.

Exterminators

Many people depend on professional exterminators to keep their homes free of unwanted pests. Generally, exterminators know what they're doing, but you are the only inspector who is going to make sure your premises aren't being assaulted with harsh chemicals that will degrade the quality of life for yourself and your pets. Be sure that the service understands that you insist on an environment that's safe for all members of your family— human, feline, and canine. If your pets act sluggish or strange after the exterminator's been at work, stay alert. Many older pets will exhibit reduced appetite, increased need for water, excessive salivation, or restlessness for several hours to a day after they've received a dose of pesticide. If any of this behavior becomes marked, or if there's vomiting, get medical help.

——— DRINK THE WATER? ———

Although many people buy filters for their drinking water, municipal water supplies are held to high health standards. As a matter of fact, a water filter that isn't kept scrupulously clean will be a worse health hazard than no water filter at all.

Private water supplies, such as wells and springs, are generally not covered under municipal pollution codes and can be dangerous. Even if this water contains no harmful bacteria or chemicals, some of it is very high in various minerals. This mineral content can encourage the formation of bladder stones.

In older homes, lead pipes may deliver drinking water from the safe municipal supply to the family's water glasses and pets' drinking bowls.

If you keep water available for your pets outside, keep it fresh. Most people are aware of acid rain and its toxic effects. Whatever particulate matter there is in the air also gets into your pet's water supply outdoors. The water may look fresh, but microscopic examination would tell a different story.

Outside water dishes for pets must be removed during any spraying, then carefully cleaned before being put back into service. In this polluted day, pets that live to old age in the outdoors are truly hardy specimens to live through the chemical assaults to which their bodies are exposed.

Similarly, if you're spraying for insects inside, remove pets' water dishes so the spray particles won't contaminate them.

Many dogs and cats drink out of the toilet bowl. This is never a good idea, as several intestinal bacteria are passed from human to animal. Further, many people use continuous cleaning agents in their toilet tanks, and having pets drink whatever chemicals keep the toilet bowl sparkling clean isn't the best health regime in the world. No one knows exactly what several years of such a beverage will do to a pet.

——— PARASITE CONTROL ———

Among the chemicals pet owners choose to bring into their lives are the various products necessary for parasite control. These pests include both the external parasites such as fleas and ticks that get on our pets and into our homes, and the internal parasites—various kinds of worms, chiefly—our pets are prey to.

These products come in many forms: powders, sprays, aerosol foggers, dips, tablets, and liquids to put on the skin. Products are also available to attack these pests in our yards. Read all labels and directions carefully, including directions on how to dispose of the empty container.

It seems nearly impossible to keep our pets without using these toxins, but as our pets get older, more discretion must be used. It's common to hear people say their old dog doesn't seem to feel very good for a few days after the application of some kind of insecticide. This should alert the owner to the need to change insecticides. The old pet is no longer up to that particular product. Also, be especially careful in the simultaneous use of several of these products. They often have much more harsh and even deadly results used together than they do alone.

Dealing with Fleas

Optimum nutrition is a cornerstone of flea control. Without it, there is little hope of control. With it, we can control fleas on pets with one of the pyrethrin sprays, plus using another product to spray our yards. Most of the fleas are not located on our pets; they're found in the environment, both inside and out.

Insect growth regulators are a non-toxic additive to some

sprays. These help in breaking the life cycle of the flea, and as they are not toxic to animals or people, they are very useful in treating carpets, furniture, and cars.

Flea Trap

To tell whether there are many fleas inside your home, build a flea trap. Place a sheet of white paper on the floor and put a pie pan about two-thirds full of water on the paper. Add a squirt of dish washing detergent and mix it in the water. At night place a small reading lamp directly over the pan. Check your trap in the morning. From one to several hundred dead fleas may be found, depending on the population in the carpet. Obviously, the more fleas you trap, the more you need to go on some program of flea eradication.

Check for Ticks

Most products that control fleas on your pets also control ticks. However, in this time of wide concern about the spread of Lyme

Flea trap

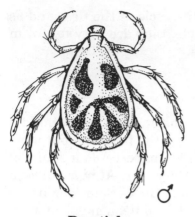

Dog tick

Engorged tick

disease, which people get from ticks, you'll be smart to check your dog or cat thoroughly after it's been outside, especially in brushy country. While there are several tick-repellent products to use before you walk in the woods or fields, another going over afterwards may save everybody a lot of pain and sickness.

Some of the ticks that carry Lyme disease are tiny, others are easily seen, and an engorged tick is especially easy to find. There is mounting evidence that dogs may suffer from Lyme disease as well as carry the ticks. Cats, too, carry ticks. This is not a subject for panic nor for utterly abandoning walks in the woods; precautions are available, and care must be taken.

How to Remove Ticks

The folklore about removing ticks is abundant—and mostly wrong. If you find a tick on your pet or yourself, use tweezers to grasp the tick as close to the head as possible. (Special forceps are available for removing ticks, should you think tweezers aren't adequate.) Then, with one smooth motion, pull the tick off.

Using an antiseptic on the spot after removing the tick can't hurt. However, since the spirochete that causes Lyme disease goes into the bloodstream, topical applications won't help. Burn the tick to make sure it won't be around to bite anyone else. Some health officials suggest that any ticks you pull off yourself or your pets should be kept in a sealed bottle for future lab tests in case you've contracted Lyme disease.

Flea Collars

You'll note that we haven't discussed flea collars as viable parasite eradicators. Most customers are dissatisfied with them. Electronic flea collars which emit a sound disliked by fleas are available. These are expensive, and many dogs wearing them still have fleas. Nor is there data yet about what years of living with the electronic emissions does to the dog. There is one place, though, where regular flea collars are helpful. Cut up a flea collar and put it in the new vacuum cleaner bag every time you change the bag. Then, when flea eggs hatch in your vacuum cleaner bag, they won't flourish.

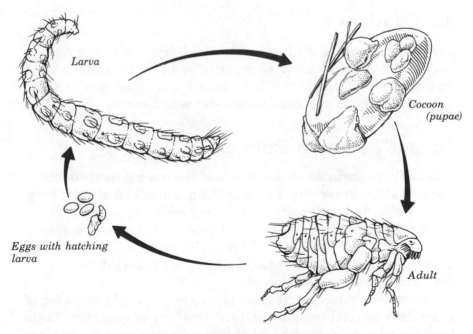

Larva

Cocoon (pupae)

Eggs with hatching larva

Adult

Life cycle of the flea

Wormers

Another group of chemicals that may be necessary to use occasionally are the wormers. The frequency of use and the products necessary vary not only with the individual pet, but with different geographical areas. Veterinarians have available the latest products, which are both highly effective and very safe. No old animal can handle a parasite burden, so get it taken care of as soon as possible.

A word of caution: Antique-type wormers are available in every grocery store and shop where pet supplies are sold. Avoid these. Most don't work effectively, and many can make your pet very ill.

A man once took a puppy with a broken leg to his veterinarian. Upon being questioned, he said he had gotten a wormer from the feed store and given it to the pup. The poor puppy got so sick that it fell off the porch and fractured the leg.

Be Cautious

With all the toxins we invite into our living areas, we need to use those that are most effective and least traumatic. Used judiciously, chemicals can help in all our lives, people's and pets'. Knowledge and caution are the watchwords.

Bigger Pollution Problems

Studies have surfaced on the effects of electric magnetic fields on various kinds of cancers. From 1979 on, papers on electric magnetic fields and especially extra-low-frequency, or ELF, fields have been published and disputed internationally. The controversies over ELF facilities in Wisconsin, upstate New York, the Upper Peninsula of Michigan, and upper Cape Cod, to name a few, are by no means resolved.

However, extensive studies not only of people but also of laboratory animals give unsettling evidence of negative effects from frequencies once thought so low as to be negligible in their impact. Effects range from increased stress all the way to elevated levels of leukemia and other forms of cancer. Where we live in relation to the lines that bring power to our homes is apparently a factor in our health and well-being, as it is also for our pets. Awareness of this can give you clues you and your veterinarian might otherwise miss when you're figuring out why an older pet is showing strange symptoms.

The entire issue of pollutants we do not individually choose to surround ourselves with is enormous and has health and public policy ramifications far beyond what any one book could begin to cover. Questions such as what poisons should be sprayed on forest lands to control the growth of unwanted species of plants or insects cause raging battles all around the country. Evidence suggests that people and pets are adversely affected by many of these chemicals. People who live or have lived in areas where nuclear weapons have been tested are wrestling with unanswered questions about why they and their animals, both pet and farm, show adverse effects far above what can be considered normal.

Conscientious individuals who want to have themselves and their animals live the best quality lives they can manage should be prudent about the pollutants that they invite into their lives, weighing benefits against possible unknown health costs. As far as pollutants that they do not personally invite into their lives, their own involvement with those who set public policy is their best line of defense. Life has never been guaranteed as entirely risk-free; however, it would appear reasonable that people should have the opportunity to make informed decisions about the risks they want themselves and, by extension, their pets, to run.

——— SIGNS OF POISONING ———

It is tricky in the extreme to diagnose poisoning in a pet, but concerned owners should be aware of some signs that may indicate poisoning so they'll know when immediate medical help must be enlisted. Some poisons kill in a matter of minutes; others take hours to cause death, and still others take days even to cause symptoms. Added to the difficulty in diagnosing a case of poisoning is the fact that one needs to know both what poison is the culprit, how much, as well as the condition of the pet prior to the poisoning incident.

It is so difficult to differentiate symptoms of various kinds of poison reactions that experts are often baffled in their diagnoses. One of the most useful things the pet owner can provide is a complete history of what happened. What kinds of poisons were available to the pet? These include:

Rodent poisons—rats, mice, gophers, moles, bats
Insecticides
Paints—lead poisoning
Fertilizers
Poisonous plants
Petroleum products
Cleaning products
Spoiled food/garbage
Poisoned carcasses

The more exact you can be in reporting what was available, the better the chances of quick, correct diagnosis and hence effective treatment. Not all poisonings will be lethal, but all must be taken seriously. It's helpful if you can take in a sample or a label from what you think your pet may have gotten into. Also, if the pet produces urine or feces before you go to the doctor, take specimens. They can hasten the diagnosis.

Physical signs of poisoning not only vary in their intensity, but also they may mimic signs of other problems not necessarily life-threatening. Thus the pet owner is faced with the problem of deciding whether this is a crisis. The older the pet, the more one needs to put time on one's side. Any veterinarian would prefer that you take your pet in too early than too late.

If you know your pet has swallowed a toxin within the last half-hour to one hour and if the label on the toxin container doesn't say not to do this, give the pet a spoonful or two of household hydrogen peroxide. It will usually cause vomiting within ten minutes and may prevent absorption of the poison. Do not give this after signs of poisoning are present without asking your veterinarian.

Signs of Poisoning

Here are some signs that often indicate poisoning. The list isn't exhaustive, and often one sign by itself isn't conclusive evidence, but if several are present or if there's a question, get help fast:

> Vomiting
> Excessive salivation
> Diarrhea
> Hypothermia (low temperature)
> Lying around listlessly
> Nervousness, restlessness
> Convulsions
> Abdominal pain
> Unexplained trembling
> Bloody fluid in mouth, nostrils
> Incontinence of bowels, urine
> Anorexia
> Altered disposition, especially irritability
> Bloody bowels, urine

Contradictory Signs

Several of these signs are contradictory. In some kinds of poisonings, the animal can go through a series of apparently contradictory signs, which is one of the things that makes diagnosis so difficult. And there are emotional signs, like the altered disposition or depression, that are highly subjective, even further complicating matters.

The confounding nub of diagnosing poisoning is that there aren't one or two conclusive signs that will tell a person, "Ah. Poisoning. Must rush to the veterinarian." However, the longer and more closely one has lived with an older pet, the more attuned one is to its normal functioning and behavior. This makes it somewhat easier to say with some certainty, "There are signs here that make me very much suspect that my pet has been poisoned, and I need help right now."

To underscore the point that even food in excess can cause some kinds of toxicity, consider Starbuck, the greedy weimaraner. A guest left a five-pound box of excellent chocolates on the dining room table as a surprise to the family when they returned from a graduation ceremony. Starbuck, however, decided to take care of the chocolates since he'd been excluded from the graduation. When the family returned, they found a sick weimaraner—abdomen tender, depressed mood, restless. They also found three or four chocolates left in a five-pound box on the floor.

Diagnosis was easy. And in a couple of days, Starbuck was back to his normal crafty self, although it is reported that he adamantly refused chocolates for many months thereafter.

Starbuck was one lucky dog, for chocolates can be toxic in large doses, especially to smaller animals.

CHAPTER
7

Unorthodox Therapies

Everyone involved in treating an older pet must keep this in mind always: There is less room for error when an aging animal gets sick than when a young, vital one does. There isn't time to play around, to wait and see, and to experiment with untested therapies.

As one veterinarian put it succinctly, "When you see blood on the floor, it isn't the time to go out in the herb garden to see what you can find that might help."

We will give you an overview of three major alternative therapies—homeopathy, acupuncture, and herbalism—and some examples of their success.

Veterinarians who practice any of these branches of therapy have completed the same education as veterinarians who do not use these. The vets who have chosen to go further than the standard education can offer their patients methods often beyond the standard orthodoxies. These methods are a case of "also," not necessarily "instead of."

Further, anyone practicing homeopathy, acupuncture, or

herbalism should be a veterinarian or should be working closely
with a veterinarian, so there is someone who will be objectively
monitoring the progress.

None of these alternative therapies lends itself to do-it-yourself diagnosis or treatment. Each is very exacting, and an un-
skilled practitioner is worse than no practitioner at all, for an
owner can be given false hope and delay getting effective treatment.

With all these warnings firmly in place, we will also stress
that when you're working with a licensed veterinarian, you can
trust that the vet isn't practicing quackery. Very simply, there
are so many veterinarians today that a quack wouldn't last long;
competition from ethical professionals would drive the person
out of business. You may find a vet who isn't very good at
medicine, but it's highly unlikely you will find one who is an
outright fraud. However, make sure that any alternate therapies you choose are at least done by someone under a vet's
supervision.

The Less the Better

We feel that the less medicine needed to maintain health, the
better for the animal. This is especially true in the aging animal
whose ability to detoxify has decreased and whose body systems
seem to be in a more delicate balance. This is also not the time to
get fanatical or obsessed with ideas, but to let common sense
prevail.

For example, if you have raised your pet on commercial foods
for many years, but recently read that alfalfa sprouts and wheat
grass are a shortcut to enlightenment, don't put fourteen-year-
old Rex on a diet of wheat grass and alfalfa sprouts. Instead, add
a bit of each to the diet that his system has become used to over
the years. These two substances are energy-packed foods, but
trying to make such a major change in the diet will cause
horrible consequences. Make changes slowly even when you go
in a positive direction so the effects will be gradual and permanent.

Frequently people get involved with alternative therapies when either a human or an animal friend is afflicted with an incurable disease such as cancer. Often, by the time the alternative therapy is tried, the disease is so advanced that nothing will cure it, and the owner of the pet then says of the alternative therapy, "Oh, that's just quackery. It didn't save my Fluffy."

Alternative therapies are medical, not miraculous. Begun at a point when the animal's body still has some ability to fight back, they may, in addition to other therapies, either hasten a cure or at least retard the progress of the disease. The lesson is to treat a problem quickly, whatever method is chosen, before the tired old organs are overwhelmed and the systems start to fail like a row of falling dominoes.

One word of hope here. Even though a condition may not be curable, often something can be done to modify the situation. Palliation is treating with the idea of improving the quality of life while knowing that no cure is possible. Many times we start treatment at this stage. For many owners of aging pets with chronic conditions, palliation is very welcome. It adds months or years of comfortable, decent-quality life for a pet who might otherwise either suffer or have to be euthanized.

If your pet is very ill, by all means use standard medicine, unorthodox treatments, or whatever else you have available. However, it is mandatory that everyone involved knows the totality of the situation, so conflicts don't arise. The ideal situation is when your veterinarian, who has been well educated in standard medical practices, has added to his or her education one or more of the less orthodox therapies and has become proficient in its use. This allows your veterinarian to choose the best from both worlds.

The therapies we'll discuss are whole fields in their own right. We want to alert you to what's available and which are most easily used on animals. Nor is this list definitive, as we deal only with those alternative therapies with which we're familiar and comfortable. We're not minimizing the effectiveness of whatever therapies we omit. In fact, we welcome additional information from any of our readers about other therapies so they might be added to future editions of this book.

————— HOMEOPATHY —————

Homeopathy is a system of medicine that originated about two hundred years ago in Germany. Its founder, Samuel Hahnemann, based the system on the principle of "Let likes be treated by likes." That is, a substance that produces symptoms when given in a large dose will cure similar symptoms if administered in minute doses.

Homeopathy is widely used in other areas of the world, especially Europe and India. Although it had a large following in America in the late nineteenth and early twentieth centuries, it lost favor for a number of years. Recently it has made a resurgence, and now homeopaths are becoming fairly commonplace across the United States.

Homeopathy can be prescribed on many levels, depending on the knowledge and experience of the practitioner. First aid kits are available (see Appendix) from many sources. Simple directions are available. Homeopathy may also be used to treat very serious problems. However, at this level, skills beyond those possessed by the average pet owner are needed. An example of this is the use of calcarea fluorica (calcium and fluorine) to help remove calcium deposits around a joint.

The medicines used in homeopathy are produced in homeopathic pharmacies. They are available all over the world.

Three big advantages these medicines have are:

1 They are quite inexpensive.

2 They are given orally in a sugar base, so they are very palatable.

3 They are non-toxic due to the minute amounts of the original substance present.

The medicines are made from every conceivable substance in nature, including plants, animals, and minerals. For example, arnica, commonly used for bruises, is made from a plant called leopard's bane. A calendula solution will hasten the healing of minor lacerations. *Crotalus horridus* (usually the Latin form is used for the names) is made from rattlesnake venom. *Natrum muriaticum*, a very common remedy in human medicine, is made from table salt. It is often amazing to see the results of treatment when these seemingly bizarre substances are homeopathically prepared and administered.

We have seen grossly swollen sprained joints become normal within twenty-four hours following one dose of homeopathically prepared *Rhus toxicodendron*, better known as poison oak.

An extensive pug kennel has been able to reduce its high rate of Caesarian births to nearly zero by giving a few doses of caulophyllum, a plant commonly called blue cohosh.

Cats crying incessantly with the severe pain of a full-blown case of bladder infection have curled up for a nap five minutes after a dose of cantharis, a preparation made of a blister-producing beetle found in Europe and Asia and sometimes called Spanish fly.

Kelly, a yellow Lab, has a malignant tumor on a bone of one front leg. Although the tumor is very obvious, the size of a large orange, and even though it has been growing very slowly, Kelly has been doing well. She walks on the leg and apparently has been pain-free for a year. She has been taking daily doses of homeopathically prepared cadmium sulphate. Hers is not a case of cured cancer, but it demonstrates how palliation can improve the quality of life for a pet otherwise doomed to amputation or severe pain.

Success Stories

Here are some other examples of successful homeopathic treatments:

Prince, an old Lab, was so terrified of loud noises that he once burrowed his way through the mattress on his owner's bed to try to get away from the sound of fireworks. Prior to his treatment, Prince was a dog totally out of control. One dose of phosphorus calmed him down so much that he weathered a Fourth of July with no problems. His improvement lasted a year. The dosage was repeated then, and Prince finished his life as a calm dog his owner could live with happily.

Ruby, a shepherd cross, had multiple fistulated tracks that

were draining pus. Two surgeries to find the cause of these infections were unsuccessful, and antibiotics did nothing to control the infection. Using homeopathically prepared silica, Ruby's veterinarian healed the fistulas in a week.

Several old females showing the kind of incontinence that causes them to leak urine during their sleep were treated with causticum, a preparation of sulfuric acid. Two or three doses of this remedy cured the problem. We suggest that this treatment is far preferable to the standard method of treatment, DES, which has many side effects.

Bounce, an older German shepherd, was getting very deaf. After a treatment with silica, his hearing improved, and the improvement lasted for several years.

The fact that homeopathy must be prescribed on an individual basis might be called a disadvantage. However, it's also a strong point in that your pet is being very carefully assessed on the points of what it needs. For example, two dogs with ear infections may need different medicines depending on the way each demonstrates the problem.

ACUPUNCTURE

Another healing art that has recently been "discovered" in the United States is acupuncture. Actually, it is thousands of years old and originated in the Orient. It has great capabilities as a healing system, handling all manner of diseases from simple to complex, but its disadvantage is that results are directly related to the knowledge and skill of the practitioner.

Acupuncture is used mainly for muscular-skeletal problems by veterinarians today, and its results may be quite startling. We have seen dogs with arthritis that weren't helped by medication become quite normal following a few treatments.

Acupuncture can also be used for internal problems such as heart, kidney, or liver failure. Some success has been reported in using acupuncture in cases of nerve damage.

It Works

Cases of pets successfully treated by acupuncture include these:

Shep, an Australian shepherd, had two major problems. Not only did he have front leg lameness that interfered with his herding activities, he also had a vicious disposition. He had to be muzzled when treated. Both his lameness and his viciousness improved after acupuncture, the latter so much so that muzzles were no longer needed.

Heidi, a Doberman, was what is commonly known as a "wobbler," a dog that suffers from vertebral instability to the point that it drastically affected her gait. Orthopedic surgeons wanted to operate on Heidi's spine, but her owner decided to try acupuncture. For her first acupuncture session, Heidi had to be carried into the doctor's office. She walked out, and after several more sessions, Heidi walked normally for the rest of her life.

Acupuncture is totally non-toxic, as no medicine is administered. Another advantage is that there's no cost for medicine. It's unlikely that the average pet owner can practice acupuncture on his or her pets. But consider yourself fortunate if you live within driving distance of a competent veterinary acupuncturist, for this person can do wonders for the aches and pains frequently seen in aging pets.

—— HERBAL MEDICINE ——

This is another very old, well-validated system of medicine, and is probably the most common system of healing used by non-industrialized people in the world today. Herbal medicine started in the Orient as an organized system.

The owner who eases her mother dog's labor by using an infusion of raspberry leaves in a tea is using herbal medicine, as is the owner who takes the sting out of a cut by treating it with the juice from a freshly broken *Aloe vera* leaf or gives his cat greens to help pass hair balls.

Other herbal preparations that have been proven include:

Comfrey, for healing bones.

Glycoflex, a product containing green-lipped mussels, is good for arthritis.

Mullein, for reproductive problems.

Peppermint, for gastro-intestinal problems, especially gas.

Spirulina and chlorella, for anemia.

Valerian root, for sedation.

Echinacea, an immune stimulant.

Materials Are Cheap

A major advantage of herbal medicine is that the raw materials are usually cheap and very plentiful. Some people grow their own; for the rest, health food stores or herbal supply companies provide a ready source of materials. Herbal preparations lend themselves to the treatment of chronic conditions in our pets.

There are drawbacks. First, thorough knowledge is required to prescribe the proper combination of herbs for a given problem. The person seeking to acquire this knowledge needs to be able to differentiate between solid facts and wishful thinking.

In this field, Mark Twain's comment applies; people often know a whole lot of things that aren't true. However, the persistent person can gradually amass a truly useful body of knowledge. Of the therapies discussed here, herbalism is the one that lends itself best to mastery on an out-student basis.

Still, the caution applies: Don't rely on your own budding knowledge of herbalism to treat an old pet instead of taking it to your vet.

A second disadvantage of herbal medicine is that many of the remedies are quite nasty tasting. This can be overcome by putting the herbs in capsules or buying them already in this form. Some of the externally applied herbal remedies smell pretty foul, too. The pet being treated with one of these concoctions will probably be banned from the living room sofa.

Finally, quality is often questionable, as one cannot be sure how long the herbs have been on the shelf. This isn't a problem if you gather fresh herbs and make the medicine up as it is needed. With herbs, as with cooking spices, the one-year rule of freshness is very important. For many herbs, even a year is too long.

A herbalist is a fine friend to have, either in human or book form. Much lore can be gleaned from people who have remained close to their roots. Your pet can be healthier and happier, too, if you gather herbal lore. We've listed a few dependable herbalists in the references.

The major advantage of starting any one or a combination of the three alternative therapies on an older pet is that none is harsh or abrupt. Thus you're not giving a big jolt to your pet's body. Often the introduction of homeopathic remedies or certain herbs as your pet is first showing signs of old age will let you slow that aging process and make it a lot easier on your pet—a kind of growing old gracefully.

CHAPTER
8

Knowing When It's the End

In the best of all worlds, our old pet goes to bed one night and dies peacefully in its sleep. More commonly, we as pet owners are faced with an agonizing decision: Is my pet's life of such painful quality that euthanasia is the kindest thing that can be done?

The decision is made more difficult emotionally because in our highly civilized society few of us see death very often, and much less often are we responsible for the death of another creature.

When we acquire a pet, we take on the total responsibility for its care throughout its life. This is beneficial for the animal, as there is less stress in providing for food and shelter than if it were out on its own.

In more natural circumstances nature takes care of the demise of the creatures. Nature is very efficient, but by our standards, not always humane: Death usually occurs from starvation or attacks by predators. We have the opportunity to end our pets' lives rapidly, but with that opportunity comes the weight of the responsibility, with all its emotional ramifications. Thoughts like "Maybe another doctor could have saved him," or "If I had only done such and such" commonly occur.

To some degree these can be prevented by gathering as much information as possible about the condition of the pet, the possible treatment programs, their potential results, their costs in money and time, what will happen if nothing is done, and, most important, answers to any questions you may have. At times like this, there are no silly questions. Most of the emotional stresses are caused by our lack of information about some aspect of the process of dying. With information, we can make rational decisions; without it, we react emotionally.

The decision to euthanize a pet depends on individual cases. Your veterinarian can help you, but you are your pet's final arbiter. There are many who believe that a humane death to end suffering is the final gift we owe our pets.

Too Early for Euthanasia

Some people believe that the loss of a leg is sufficient reason to put a pet to death. More often than not, that isn't true. Amputation of a limb is basically harder for an owner to think about than it is for most pets to cope with. Many people have been taught to be embarrassed about a missing limb. Animals don't know they're supposed to be embarrassed, so they're not.

Tiffany, a black Great Dane, had a fast-moving cancer that her veterinarian felt necessitated amputating her front leg. After consultation with another veterinarian whose expertise was with Danes, her owners were able to make an educated decision. Yes, the amputation would arrest the cancer, at least for a time, and yes, the Dane could enjoy a good quality of life on three legs.

Subsequently a passer-by could see Tiffany carrying her Frisbee proudly. She no longer leaped into the air after it, but she insisted on her own sedate version of chase-the-Frisbee for several years after her amputation. Her family learned to take her three-legged condition as part of life and enjoyed Tiffany's companionship.

Life in Her Eyes

Stella, another black Great Dane, was taken into a Humane Shelter weighing less than forty pounds and with a front foot that was gangrenous from having been in a steel trap for perhaps two weeks. The owner's agent, who had been supposed to be looking after Stella, was called and went to the shelter to look at her. Deciding she was too far gone to be saved, he told the shelter personnel to have her put to death.

But something about Stella alerted the chief kennel person, who called a Dane breeder to look at her. Stella was emaciated, and her foot was an evil-smelling mess. But there was life in her eyes. A veterinarian felt that she had a chance under proper care, and she got that chance. Though she lost two toes to the trap, with antibiotics, dressings, and highly nutritious food, Stella not only recovered, but through an amazing chain of circumstances, was reunited with her owner a year later. The lack of two toes doesn't affect her balance, and she's happily watching after her owner's family.

Stella exemplifies that subtle nuance that some people can pick up and others miss. The chief kennel person felt that she wasn't a dog that ought to be put to death, and he was right. The owner's agent perhaps saw only the ruin of the sleek, fine Dane he'd been supposed to care for, and would have had her killed.

Difficult for Owner

Old age isn't always pretty, just as injuries aren't pretty. It is sometimes hard for an owner to look at a pet that once was sleek and beautiful but now is creaky, maybe has a dull, scraggly coat, and perhaps often soils the carpet. Whether that owner should have the pet put to death doesn't call for a cut-and-dried answer.

Maybe the owner can learn to love what Robert Frost called "a diminished thing." Maybe because the owner is so put off by what's become of a once-vital pet, it would be better for the pet to be put down than to suffer being ignored and maybe even despised. Each of us has to answer in our own way.

Newt is a creaky, ugly eighteen-year-old Chihuahua with a big tumor on her shoulder. Her owners continue to spend lots of money to have their veterinarian treat the tumor. Newt is mostly deaf, spends much of her life sleeping on her pillow, and goes hysterical if you surprise her. She's not a whole lot different than she ever was, as her owners point out. She was never either a beauty or a charmer. She's creaking around, eating well and having about as much fun as she ever had. Her owners see no reason to abbreviate her life just because there are younger, more beautiful dogs in the world.

Quality of Life

That phrase "quality of life" must become more than a catch-phrase when we think about how our old pets are doing with their lives. Like old people, old pets know some things are different, and many times an old pet is embarrassed by some of those changes. A once-clean house dog does truly despise losing bowel or bladder control, and it may become a kindness to free that dog from its unhappiness with its embarrassing predicament. A cat that once leapt lithely from chair back to stair rail but who now is tottering around and floor-bound will show you that it is unhappy with its diminished life.

A woman who had an old black Lab cross, Brahms, returned from a cross-country business trip to find that Brahms was barely able to get up on his feet to greet her at the excellent kennel where she'd left him.

She carried him home, made him a special, soppy meal, carried him outside to do his eliminations, and took time off from work to try to bring him through his dire condition.

In tears she called, asking whether his condition definitely warranted her having him euthanized. How can one tell, cross-country? But, reminded gently that what she needed to consider above everything else, her own grief included, was the quality of Brahms's life, she took him to his vet the next morning and had him put down. She sent a terse telegram: "The quality wasn't there anymore."

Act in Kindness

Thus there are situations when kindness and consideration for the pet simply demand that we make the terminal decision. Caesar, another black Dane, was walking stiffly at age eight. X-rays showed such degeneration of his hip sockets that bone was rubbing on bare bone at every step he took. After consultation with the veterinarian, who said that such a condition was horribly painful and would only get worse, Caesar's owner decided that love for the dog demanded that he be euthanized even before he came out of the anaesthesia he'd been given prior to the revealing X-rays.

Killer, a blue Dane, had a nasty tumor on his shoulder that resisted treatment and was causing him pain. While the dog was on the operating table, his vet made a slide from the tumor, put it under a microscope, opened a text to pictures of cancerous cells, and then asked the owner, who was present at the surgery, to compare Killer's slide with the text.

The owner studied the slide carefully, comparing what he was seeing with the text.

"OK," he said. "It's clear what's going on. I want to be there while you put him down."

Like most owners in such circumstances, he bawled.

Trying to Push Too Far

There are times when we don't recognize the seriousness of a condition and would continue trying for treatment past the time when it will be beneficial. There are many medical aspects to be considered in these cases. These should be discussed with your veterinarian, who should be philosophically in agreement with you on the subject of euthanasia. Some vets will euthanize an animal long before it's necessary, and some wait too long, so be sure you both think alike at this time.

There are many questions to clear up at this time, depending on your knowledge of the situation. Realities are what everyone involved is trying to ascertain. If you want your fifteen-year-old cat, for instance, with end-stage kidneys to last until next spring when the kids get out of school, you will be setting yourself up for disappointment.

A feeding stand helps this older dog.

Ask the vet if he can cure the problem, greatly slow the process, palliate (make the pet comfortable), or offer no hope at all. If there is nothing further that can be done, the decision becomes clear. If the problem can be solved or the process slowed, you probably have a temporary reprieve on the decision of whether to euthanize. Use the time wisely. It won't last forever.

Once you have the prognosis, you can direct your questions to the veterinarian more accurately. And you can perhaps become more at peace with your own decision, whatever it may be.

Accepting that the end is here isn't easy, even when you're

fairly well informed about prognoses. The owner was clinging so hard to her ten-year-old bulldog that she considered having him operated on again for bladder stones. She was lucky that she had a long and honest relationship with her veterinarian.

"How long does that poor dog have to live" the vet asked, "to fulfill your idea of what's long enough?"

She understood what he was telling her and had the dog euthanized that very day.

Speaking for the pet that can't speak for itself is what people that care about pets do. Sometimes it's the owner, sometimes it's the veterinarian, sometimes it's both in chorus. Seldom is it easy.

Be Alert to Signals

If you can pay attention, most pets give clear indications when they don't want to live any longer. Tiger Paws, a deaf sixteen-year-old cat, began hanging around inside the house, demanding to be held one Monday. By Tuesday, he looked as if he'd lost five pounds and his coat was dull. He drank water and a little milk, but he wasn't his normal piggy, independent self. By afternoon, he was clearly going rapidly downhill.

His owner took him to the veterinarian and said, "I think Tiger Paws is close to death. I don't want him to suffer."

The veterinarian examined Tiger Paws and agreed. It was only a matter of seconds for the shot to take effect. Probably Tiger would have died naturally in the next few days or so, but his going would have been hard, for he never did anything the easy way. This time, though, he'd made it clear that he wasn't ready to go down the road much farther. As his advocate, with the help of a veterinarian, his owner made that one event easy for Tiger.

Your pet will give you indications that the end is near. These are usually subjective, but when coupled with objective evidence, they are valuable. All the signs are a variation of a loss of awareness of or interest in the pet's surroundings. This will eventually include the people it has been associated with for so long.

One of the first signs is an increase in sleeping. Sometimes it is difficult to awaken the animal. Another sign may be an inclination to eliminate in the house or very close to the sleeping area. This will progress to defecation and urination in the animal's bed. Loss of appetite and finally even disinterest in water consumption indicate that death will occur within a day or so.

These signs are usually what we see in a relatively normal death of an animal. Many of these will just die in their sleep. When a more violent illness is occurring near the end of a pet's life, there may be more evidence of pain, as well as vomiting, diarrhea, respiratory distress, and more emotional signs such as whining, crying, or excessive restlessness. These are animals for whom we often feel the need to end their suffering before nature takes its course.

The Choice is Clear

It's no easier for a veterinarian to put a pet to death than it is for the owner. Veterinarians are healers and helpers of pets, not executioners. But there are times when the good of the pet demands that the end be recognized.

When major parts of systems stop functioning, as for instance kidneys no longer are able to remove toxins from the system, the choice for the pet is either slow death from uremic poisoning or a quick death by euthanasia. If lungs are filled with fluid and the pet's every breath is an agony, cure isn't going to happen. If a pet has lost total bowel and bladder control, neither medication nor surgery can reverse that condition. The key here is that something vital has worn out due to age or disease. We do not transplant organs as often on pets as we're doing more and more often on people, so the worn-out part can't be replaced.

If it seems your pet is nearing the end, and usually we are aware of this, even though we may try to deny the evidence, have a serious talk with your veterinarian and with other members of the family. It doesn't work well if one member of the family takes the pet in for euthanasia without consultation or consent from other members. Many long-lasting problems with trust and resentment can result from such an action.

Whether to discuss euthanasia with children depends on the age, the emotional state of the child, and your own beliefs. In general, children who are accurately informed deal well with death, but you must make your own decision. Incomplete information such as "I'm taking Fluffy to the vet to put him to sleep" can produce all sorts of extremely negative reactions towards the veterinarian, the parents, and even sleep itself by children who don't get the whole story.

Injections Given

In the euthanasia process, generally animals are given an intravenous injection of a concentrated anesthetic product specifically made for euthanasia. The animal usually expires within one minute after the injection. Pets who have had good health care all their lives have no dread of the injection. For them, this is another shot among the many they've had in their lives.

Discuss beforehand whether you wish to be present. If you want to and the vet doesn't allow it, find someone else or get your vet to make an exception. You have the right to attend. You will have to allow the doctor and the staff to do their job efficiently, which usually means that the doctor's assistant will hold the animal. The doctor doesn't want to miss the vein because the animal isn't properly restrained. However, you're generally allowed to touch the pet during the process.

Many people elect to say good-bye to the pet and then leave the rest to the veterinarian. In any event, have the process done according to your wishes, don't be embarrassed if tears flow—it's very normal—and realize that because you've become well informed, you are making the best decision possible for your pet.

Burial should be considered before euthanasia and discussed with your vet. Several possibilities exist, depending on local laws and your own wishes. Many areas have burial services that will bury your pet. Some have pet cemeteries; some don't. Some offer cremation. In some areas you may bury your pet on your own property if you want to.

Finally, attention must be given to you and to other family members, especially being alert to the presence of abnormal grief. That is grief that lasts too long or seems to be excessive. This can occur especially with children or people who have no other family except the pet who has just been euthanized. There are grief counselors available in many parts of the country. If there are none in your area, get some good professional assistance. Our emotional attachment to animals can sometimes be stronger than it is to other people, and a lot of emotional stress may occur after the death of a pet, especially when euthanasia is involved.

We don't—fortunately—always have to make the hard decision. Some pets slip gently out of life, never having had pain or illness, answering some decision of their own.

Those are the easy ones.

CHAPTER
9

Preparing Your New Pet for Old Age

After you've lost a pet, whether you choose to get another is one of those highly individual decisions that goes with people's choices about how they're going to live their lives. Most people who have enjoyed a pet for many years will bring another into their lives.

The new pet won't replace the previous one. Making comparisons between the former pet and the new one may be tempting, but it works to everyone's disadvantage.

You may need time to mourn your old pet before you choose a new one. There's no right or wrong way to decide this, only what suits you best. Fill your own needs, and don't let the opinions of others dictate your behavior. Family members or friends who crowd your decision can be difficult, especially if they foist off on you a pet not of your own choosing before you're ready to take on the new responsibility. This is a time when you need to stand up for your own choices.

There may have been many changes in your life since you acquired your previous pet. You may not want a similar type of animal, even. If you had a family and a very active dog but are now living alone in a small apartment, perhaps a cat or a small dog would be more appropriate. You also don't have to start over with a puppy or a kitten. Adult dogs and cats are available for adoption, and these usually fit in just fine after a short period of adjustment. If you have become physically less able, perhaps a tank of tropical fish or a bird would be a good choice. With careful consideration of your status, you can make the appropriate choice.

This chapter is written for the people who decide to replace their dog or cat with a puppy or a kitten. It will provide them with information that will benefit a younger pet. While some of the items included may seem very simple and matters of common sense, you must realize that the simple things done early eliminate the need for more drastic measures later. Anything that can reduce stress in an animal's early life gives that animal a better chance to handle problems later on.

——— THE IDEAL START ———

Getting your pet ready for old age should start before it is even conceived. If you have influence with the breeding parents, you can make the odds favor you. Breeding two dogs or cats whose ancestors have been healthy and lived long, happy lives doesn't guarantee what you'll get in the offspring, but it surely improves your chances of having long-lived healthy offspring, especially if these kittens or puppies get the good care they deserve for the duration of their lives.

The prospective mother should be in good physical condition. Providing good nutrition for her and her coming litter is vital to the health of all concerned. This doesn't mean all the food the expectant mother can eat. It does mean a diet that provides for the increased requirements of the pregnancy plus the mother's daily maintenance.

A common misunderstanding is that you must feed huge amounts of food during the pregnancy. This can result in an overweight, out-of-condition mother, huge puppies or kittens, and a difficult delivery. Our experience has been that expectant animal mothers seldom overeat. However, while the kittens or puppies are nursing, you'll want to provide Mom with lots of extra food, which she'll likely demand and definitely need.

Supplements?

Controversy surrounds the question of whether to supplement the mother's diet during pregnancy. The words of a successful long-time breeder of boxers are worth remembering. He said, "Those puppies are going to get all the calcium they need from somewhere. If you don't put it into the mother's diet, they'll get it from her."

Especially with the giant breeds of dogs, careful calcium supplementation is vital; become knowledgeable on this subject.

Equally controversial is the question of whether to add vitamin C to the pregnant mother's diet. Since publication of the canine studies on the efficacy of vitamin C in minimizing hip dysplasia is only about fifteen years old, and since many veterinarians remain unconvinced by the studies, you must depend partly on your own convictions about vitamin C and partly on what your veterinarian thinks. Any excess vitamin C will be excreted in the urine. Vets who know a lot about nutrition urge pet owners to supplement the mother with C while she's pregnant and while she's lactating.

Moderate exercise is essential during pregnancy. This keeps the muscles in tone and gives better odds of a speedy delivery. The faster a puppy or kitten is born, the less chance there is it will suffer from a lack of oxygen to the brain.

First Eight Weeks

From birth to weaning at approximately eight weeks of age is an important period in a pet's early life. Although most of the care is provided by the mother, you should oversee the process so that everything progresses smoothly. You're still supplementing Mother, since what she's getting is passed on to her litter. You may want to supplement even the newborns with a few drops of liquid vitamins, especially the B's and vitamin C. This applies to kittens as well as to puppies.

This is the time to get puppies or kittens used to being handled by humans. Doing this will minimize the stress that sometimes occurs when a puppy or kitten is weaned without being handled. It's about like taming a wild creature, definitely no fun for pet or owner, and the effects frequently remain throughout life, with the animal always being a bit flighty. Flighty equals stress, and stress equals problems down the road.

___ ON TO THE NEW HOME ___

A puppy or kitten going to a new home creates a stressful time for the pet and the new owner. Try to make it as easy as possible on the youngster.

The pet's nutrition before you bought it should have been good, so you can continue the same diet. However, if the diet was inadequate, you can't start too soon to upgrade it. Supplements are definitely beneficial at this time. Nutrition is the most important controllable variable that a pet owner has in producing a healthy pet throughout its life.

Visit Your Veterinarian

In this post-weaning period, your young pet is most susceptible to contagious diseases. Its immunity from the mother is decreasing, and its own active immunity from vaccines has not yet

taken over. Therefore, keeping your new puppy or kitten iso-lated from diseased animals is important. Don't go to the park or dog shows to show off your new puppy. Play in your own yard and wait for a safer time to bring the young animal into contact with other animals.

As soon as possible after you get your new puppy or kitten, take it to your vet. If you don't have a vet, ask the person you got the pet from for advice, or get a referral from a friend whose pet's health you admire.

There are two reasons for this right-away trip to the vet. First, you want to make sure your pet is healthy. Reputable breeders are eager for you to do this, and if your vet finds anything wrong, a reputable breeder will replace the pet for you. However, if you wait more than forty-eight hours, your pet may have been exposed to some disease in your environment. The breeder won't want to take it back and expose the rest of the litter to whatever your pet has picked up.

On this first trip to the vet, expect your pet to be given a thorough physical exam. This will include checking its tempera-ture, listening to its heart, examining its ears, eyes, nose, and anus, checking for retained testicles in a male, looking for either severe overbite or underbite, and checking for hernias. Depend-ing on your pup's age, your vet may look for baby teeth that haven't fallen out and are blocking the emergence of adult teeth. Your vet will comment on signs of health or lack thereof in your pet—alertness, shiny coat, vitality, and healthy weight.

A fecal sample will be taken unless you've been thoughtful enough to bring one with you. This way, the vet can determine whether your pet has any internal parasites, of which round-worms are the most common, and prescribe whatever wormers are necessary. The pet will also be checked for external para-sites—mainly fleas—and you'll be given whatever you need to control these.

But, you say, I checked when I got my puppy, and it had a nice, cold nose. Isn't that enough sign that it's healthy?

Forget all the warm nose/cold nose stories. A warm nose on a puppy might mean it's been sleeping with its nose in a warm place. And a cold nose, to borrow from the late Walt Kelly, might mean it's dead.

Health Products

While we're in the "Forget It" department, also forget all the worm medications you can buy in the supermarkets. Many of the over-the-counter wormers may make your pet sick without getting rid of the worms. Worm medications work by poisoning the worms; to do this, the medication has to be more or less hard on your pet. The only way you'll know for sure that your pet is getting the medication it needs for the specific worms it has is to let your vet prescribe. Veterinarians have access to much safer worm medications than those you'd get over the counter.

The same holds true for flea preparations, although to a lesser extent. Fleas are marvelously adaptable beasts. What wiped them out last year in your area may, this year, only make them laugh. Your vet is the one who keeps up with what's working and what isn't. Save yourself and your pet time, money, and grief by asking your vet what to use.

Flea collars are the most widely sold flea product, and they also draw the most customer dissatisfaction. One reason for this is that people expect too much of them. When we look at a Great Dane and consider how much dog there is for fleas to roam around on, we laugh at the notion of fastening a flea collar around a Dane's neck and expecting it to keep the entire dog flea-free. We'd have to put a flea collar around each ankle, one around the tail, and one in the middle as a belt, as well as the one around the neck, to begin to get flea control.

It is silly, too, to expect the flea collar to do the job if your dog is roaming through fields and woods. The number of fleas and ticks your pup can accumulate in a jaunt through the forest is more than a collar can handle.

Some consider flea collars not only relatively ineffective, but also more toxic than a pet should be exposed to on a daily basis. Think about this before you put a flea collar on a small puppy or a kitten. There are other methods of flea control. Let the final word rest with your own veterinarian.

The First Shots

On this first trip to the vet's you'll discuss your pet's immunization program. If you received a record of whatever shots your pet has already had, take it along with you so your vet will know exactly what those shots were. Know your pet's age, as this influences what shots it gets.

Immunizations are controversial in regard to how many, time sequence, and what diseases to immunize against. Follow your veterinarian's recommendations. Remember, though, that vaccinations don't have much effect if given before eight weeks of age, and that each vaccine produces an effect on the body's immune system. This may or may not be a lasting negative effect. It seems irrational to vaccinate a puppy every two to three weeks starting at five weeks of age, as some advocate.

Against what diseases will your vet immunize your pup? Veterinarians use what's called DHLPP. This five-in-one shot prevents distemper, hepatitis, leptospirosis, parvovirus, and parainfluenza. These are the most common canine diseases that vets immunize against, and unless there is some unusual scourge in your area, your vet is unlikely to suggest more than the DHLPP right now—with one addition. Puppies are routinely vaccinated against the corona virus. What we're talking about are reasonable vaccines, a course that will help keep your pup healthy and guard against the big killers, without so heavily loading your pup with vaccines that its immune system is thrown for a loop. Ideally, the immunization process for your pup will start at eight weeks of age and go on with shots about once a month until sixteen weeks.

Shots for Kittens

Kittens are vaccinated against feline leukemia, distemper, and respiratory viruses. These immunizations start at eight weeks and regular booster shots should be scheduled.

In the proper time, your vet will also give your pet or kitten rabies shots. If you live in an area where heartworms are a problem, the prevention routine against heartworms for dogs will begin.

Once your vet recognizes you as a person who cares about the health of your pet, he or she will keep you posted on what you need to do next. You'll want to get booster shots as requested, but there is little rationale for annually vaccinating a twelve-year-old dog or cat for diseases such as distemper. Rabies protection should be continued throughout the life of the pet as required by law.

YOU AND YOUR
———— VETERINARIAN ————

The second reason for this first trip to your vet is that next to you, the veterinarian will to be your pet's best friend. For that to happen in the best way, you need to learn how to talk to your vet. You need to learn to take a specific set of symptoms when you go to the vet. Saying, "My pup just isn't acting right" isn't helpful. Saying, "She's missed three meals, is listless, isn't drinking water, and hasn't had a bowel movement since Tuesday" gives a specific set of symptoms.

You also need to be able to listen. If you don't understand what your vet said, ask for clarification. If your memory isn't what you once hoped it would be (and whose is?), take a small notebook with you and jot down things you need to remember. Unlike people, pets can't tell where it hurts. They need you to speak for them. When you become a knowledgeable reporter, you help your vet get to the problem more quickly.

Veterinarians know that although their training is in the treatment of animal diseases, they also must relate to the owners of those animals. If, by chance, you go to a vet who isn't willing to communicate with you, who isn't proud enough of his or her establishment to show you around, and who seems to resent your questions, look further for the person you're going to work with during the life of your pet. There's no substitute for a caring, knowledgeable veterinarian. Seek one out and listen to what is said. Whatever fees you have to pay now are money in the bank for the well-being of your new pet. The only person who can come close to the value of a good vet is a long-time breeder who has worked closely with an excellent vet.

_____ NUTRITION _____

Now that you've made sure your new pet is protected against the most common diseases, let's get back to the subject of feeding your new pet, dealing with puppies first. Most breeders believe in three meals a day until your pup is about five months old. Then, as soon as your puppy starts playing with lunch and not slicking it up in about fifteen minutes, it's time to omit lunch.

The three prepared meals will consist of a good kibble—the best you can afford—plus two additives. If you have a golden retriever or one of the larger breeds of dogs, consider a wheat-based kibble. Bloat is a problem with many dogs. Vets think that some of the causes of bloat are soy and kibbled corn, so the path of prudence is to avoid dry dog foods that have either of those ingredients listed in the first five on the side of the bag.

Additives

The two additives you should provide are a calcium/vitamin D/phosphorus powder and vitamin C. Studies released in 1976 indicate that vitamin C is vital for the development of proper connective tissue, so the correct amount of this is important, especially for good hips.

In the wild, dogs ate lots of vegetable matter and got enough vitamin C-rich foods to meet their needs. Today's domesticated dog doesn't eat that way, and as the dog can't synthesize enough vitamin C to meet the needs of a growing puppy, you need to put the vitamin C into the diet. Vitamin C is vitamin C, so use whatever you use for yourself. However, don't give tablets to small puppies or kittens, as they can choke on them. Instead, grind them up.

The calcium/phosphorus/vitamin D powder helps develop strong bones. Be sure whatever powder you use has vitamin D in it. If it doesn't, feed cod liver oil, too, either liquid or capsules, because without the vitamin D, your puppy can't use the calcium. Especially in larger breeds, puppies need help in this department. No matter how much a kibble is advertised as a puppy formula, it probably doesn't contain as much available calcium as the giant puppies need. Follow the feeding directions on how much calcium to add.

In case you get a vet who doesn't believe the studies on feeding vitamin C, here's the formula we use on Danes: It's 500 milligrams until the pup is four months old. Then increase it to 1000 milligrams (one gram) until the pup is eight months old. Another increase at that time, up to two grams (2000 milligrams) will see your puppy through until it is two years old. Then you can quit, as your pup will have reached its full growth. Reduce the amounts for smaller dogs and quit when the dog is about eighteen months old, when growth is pretty much complete.

C is a safe vitamin. Too much and your pup's urine will be rich in vitamin C. However, calcium is another matter. Stay close to the exact amounts recommended. We walk a fine line here: Too little and you retard the growth of your big puppy; too much and you flirt with over-calcification, especially in the shoulder joints.

Moisten the kibble on the three prepared meals. This insures that the additives will be mixed in well. Puppies eat better when the kibble is wet. Many people, however, like puppies to have dry biscuits or dry kibble to chomp on at all times from about three months to about six months, as they teethe furiously then and the dry food gives them something legal to munch on.

How Much Food?

It's difficult to prescribe exact amounts to feed a growing puppy, as each pup grows at its own rate and eats accordingly. Another reason to keep dry food always available when you can't be home all day is that it keeps your pup from getting too hungry and hence overloading at mealtime – and serves as comfort and occupational therapy when the pup is bored or lonely.

One of the feeding mistakes many people make is to constantly change brands of kibble in the mistaken notion that such variety does a dog good. It doesn't. Instead, it upsets a dog's digestive system, causes diarrhea, and eventually produces a problem eater. Stick with the basic kibble. Provide variety by

adding pan juices, canned dog food, cooked eggs, raw vegetables, or grated cheese.

Increase your pup's food quantity as the pup seems to need more, but keep a young dog on the slender side. The notion of a roly-poly puppy just isn't right. Dogs are having a growth explosion that first year, and you don't want to burden their growing, soft bones with a layer of lard. We've found that dogs live longer if they're always on the slender side—just as we're told people do.

Kittens do very well on a premium kitten chow, plus canned food if you like. A few spoonfuls of milk are good if they don't produce diarrhea. Goat's milk, if it's available, is fine. A liquid multivitamin helps get your kitten off to a healthy life.

Stress Control and Exercise

The less stress a pet has in early life, the better off it's likely to be as an adult. Some curbing of exercise, especially during the period of seven to fifteen months of age, is indicated for puppies. With the giant breeds, males especially may be incredibly clumsy at this time, and strenuous play results in sprains and lameness. If you have older dogs, you may have to cut down the amount of time a big puppy is allowed to play with them.

With one dog, let it play at will, but don't keep a puppy playing when it's tired. Treat puppies and kittens like the babies they are, and let them sleep a lot.

Never run a puppy alongside a bicycle, or, as some dog show fanatics do, behind a car "to build muscles." That's downright cruelty, and far from building muscles, it causes great and often permanent structural problems.

Consider, too, where you are exercising your pup. A hot road is very hard on a dog's footpads. More than one dog has been taken to a vet for lameness that turned out to be footpads worn raw. If you've built up to a ten-mile jog every day, don't expect your pup to keep pace with you right from the start. Give the pup time to build up, too.

Don't Let Pup Roam

Letting a puppy roam at will, even if you live where there are miles and miles of open country with neither traffic nor neighbors, is unwise, because your puppy will never bond with you.

Dogs are basically pack animals. If you want a puppy to become your loyal pet, you and your family must become the puppy's "pack." In the litter with its mother, the pup looked to her for its needs. Now you want the puppy to turn to you. A puppy running loose comes to view you as a semi-relevant appendage that puts the food dish down–period.

Consider, too, that any dog can become a runner of sheep, cattle, chickens, or the neighbors' cats if allowed to roam freely. Further, your dog is then at the mercy of anyone who wants to hurt it–and legally in some places your roaming dog can be picked up and kept by anyone who wants to do so.

As a responsible dog owner, you owe it to everyone, dogs and people, to keep your dog on your own place. Because our world is becoming more and more crowded, the places where dogs are welcome are becoming fewer and fewer. Dog owners who refuse to keep their dogs on their own premises cause more and more restrictive laws to be passed that further narrow the places where dogs are welcome.

But most important, a restricted puppy grows up to be a people-oriented dog. By the time you've lovingly raised your puppy to adulthood, you should have a dog that prefers being near you to being anywhere else. You are the leader of your dog's pack.

Kittens should be allowed outdoors only with supervision, especially in populated areas. There are too many hazards to allow these little explorers out on their own. Although cats are solitary by nature, not pack animals like dogs, the more your kitten learns to look to you for its needs from an early age, the more closely your cat will bond with you.

Sleeping Quarters and Chills

Chills and drafts carry off more puppies than diseases do. If you will remember that, you and your puppy will be in good shape. Even the heavily coated sled dogs of the North seek shelter and warmth at night. Sleeping quarters for nighttime should be inside your house, unless you have one of the heavily coated dogs like the Siberian huskies that doesn't thrive in the indoor temperatures people like.

How can you expect a dog to guard a house if it has no stake in that house? More important, your dog is a member of the family and belongs inside at night, just like everybody else. The rule books insist on making a puppy sleep in the kitchen, laundry room, or some other unusual place. That doesn't take into account some basic matters of canine psychology, especially that a new puppy has just been separated from its normal family or pack and is seeking its new place in a social hierarchy.

If you let the puppy sleep in your bedroom at first, even on the bed if you're happy with that arrangement, when the pup gets used to being away from its litter mates and accepts you as pack leader or alpha dog, it'll find its own sleeping place. Until then, your closeness at night gets everyone off to a better start—and you won't have an unhappy, crying puppy.

Don't spend a lot of money on elaborate beds for a pup. It will tear up a few blankets or rugs or whatever you put down as bed before growing up, so you're wasting money on anything elaborate. A trip to a second-hand store will get you a sturdy blanket, and that will do fine. However, remember that big dogs need lots of cushioning. They're heavy, and sleeping on hard surfaces wears patches on their elbows.

Kittens should be kept indoors at night for their own safety, and will most likely sleep in whatever cozy, private, warm place they choose.

Outside Quarters

You'll probably want outside sleeping quarters for your dog, too. A draft-free, roomy house with the floor raised off the ground and the door offset so your dog can get out of the draft will do nicely. The dog must be able to stand up or stretch out comfortably. If you have a garage, build a wooden sleeping house inside it, with access to a fenced pen.

Make the pen wide enough so that your adult dog's tail won't hit the wire when it wags a greeting to you, or it will have a bloody tail from beating it against the fence. Don't make the pen so small that your dog is in a cage; the pen needs to be big enough so your dog can romp and dig in it. You don't need chain link fencing; a sturdy six-foot high wire mesh will do. We suggest that you use six-foot fencing no matter how small your dog is so that visiting dogs can't easily jump into the pen.

For bedding in the outside kennel, use straw, well powdered with kennel dust for flea control. Straw gives a cushioned surface, doesn't produce dust that could annoy a dog, doesn't have to be washed, doesn't get chewed up, and goes on the mulch pile when the dog is through with it.

Whether to chain a dog or build a pen for it is a matter of personal preference. Surely it is cruel to chain a dog where it is prey to every passing dog and child who might want to torment it. It is also vital that a tied or chained dog not be able to get itself wrapped up in the chain and choke. Shelter and shade must be available. We've seen too many dogs that were tied out in someone's yard and never given any sort of human companionship. One wonders why such people have a dog.

Whether you select a pen, fenced yard, or chain, common sense and compassion are among the best guides you can have. The well-managed dog that has its own spot on its owner's premises is the kind of happy, well-mannered dog that you're probably aiming for.

Collars

You'll go through several collars while your pup is growing up. Get a nylon webbing choker first. This will be soft enough to not hurt the pup, yet give you enough control to begin leash-breaking.

At some time you may need a strong, flexible chain choker, especially for rambunctious big puppies of the giant breeds. Be sure to get a wide-linked chain choker; the narrow little links of others can cut cruelly into a dog's neck. And don't let yourself be talked into the chokers that have barbs or spurs on the inside. These are cruel in the extreme.

Once your pup is dependably leash-trained, you can go back to the webbing choker if you prefer, for the training should hold, whatever the material of the collar.

Don't leave your dog unattended in a collar that the pet can't slip out of. This advice isn't whimsy. One woman was lucky enough to be present when her weimaraner caught his choker on a branch when he was jumping a fence. She boosted him on her shoulder and took the choker off before he hanged himself.

Some people who finished their Great Dane's championship on a Sunday and planned to breed him the following week never got to do that. They left his choker on when they went to work Monday and he hanged himself on the backyard fence.

Cautious people don't even leave dogs in the house unattended with chokers on because they've also heard of the many, many dogs that have hanged themselves.

Cats need as much caution about collars as dogs do—maybe even more, being the climbers and explorers that they are. Free-roaming kittens or cats shouldn't wear collars when they're out of their owners' sight, and only collars that easily pop or slip off are at all advisable.

Housebreaking Young Pets

The easiest way to begin housebreaking a puppy about six weeks old is to paper-train. Put thick layers of newspaper by the door you'll eventually use to take the puppy outdoors.

Every time it eats, wakes up from a nap, drinks, or finishes playing, take the puppy to the paper and use whatever command you're going to use to tell it to eliminate. Whatever the command is, be sure all members of the family use it, or you'll have a confused puppy. Praise the pup when it obeys. Be loud in your scolding when it squats anywhere else in the house.

Whenever you catch your pup squatting where it shouldn't, pick it up (even when it is going) and place it firmly on the paper, repeating something like "Do it on the paper." Three or four conscientious days of this and your pup will be fairly dependably paper-trained.

Never rub the dog's nose in its own excrement. Contrary to popular opinion, this nasty exercise doesn't teach housebreaking.

Paper-training is a useful first step because at night, or when you can't be at home, the pup has a legal place to go. A dog seems always to remember paper-training. If the dog is sick or the weather is such that going outside is unwise, you can revert to the paper.

Once you've gotten the paper-training well established and want to move on, watch for the dog to head for the paper. Open the door and say, "Let's go OUT," emphasizing the OUT. This second phase comes easily. A couple days of this and you'll have a housebroken pup.

A word of warning: Housebreaking doesn't necessarily carry over from one house to another at first.

Housebreaking kittens is usually easy. Show the new kitten where the litter pan is. Scratch its paws in the litter if it hasn't had a litter pan before. As with a puppy, when you see your kitten wake up from a nap, take it to the litter pan. However, since cats like privacy, don't stand around watching or your kitten may never go.

Cats or kittens don't use litter pans sometimes because the pan is dirty or too many cats are using the same pan. Some cats, too, don't like some brands of litter. If you have a problem cat, try changing the brand, and be sure the pan is clean, accessible, and private.

Once you've taught your kitten to use a litter pan, continue to provide it during the summer even if you think the weather is so nice that the cat will surely prefer to be outdoors.

Crates

If there's one way that you can tell a novice from a professional when it comes to dog owners, it's that the professional uses the crate. We described crates in the chapter on enhancing the home environment. The crate must be tall enough for the adult dog to stand up and turn around in comfortably. It must also be well ventilated and should be easy to clean.

When used properly, the crate becomes bed, safe spot, and the preferred spot for your dog when it needs to go somewhere and think. Improperly used, it becomes a prison.

For you, the crate can be the difference between being able to keep your dog or not. It also makes traveling easier and assures that you and your dog will be welcome in many more places than you might otherwise be—as with relatives with the Oriental rugs. If you decide eventually to show your dog, you'll be ahead of the game, because many professional handlers won't accept a dog that isn't crate-trained.

Using the Crate

When you get your puppy home, start by giving it treats inside the crate. Leave the door open for a few days until the puppy willingly accepts the crate as a safe place where pleasant things happen. Perhaps the best place for a crate is the kitchen, because that's where people and dogs tend to congregate.

After a few days of having your puppy home and somewhat used to the crate, take a coffee break in the kitchen. Give your pup a favorite toy in the crate and close the door. If you've done your preliminaries well, the closed door will cause no problems or panic. But if the pup fusses, give it a sharp "NO"—and leave the door closed. If the fussing continues, you may have to rap smartly on the side of the crate, again saying "NO." Make the puppy stay in the crate for a few minutes after it has quieted down, and don't make a big deal of the pup when it comes out of the crate after you've opened the door.

Every time you either give the pup something in the crate or put the pup in the crate, be sure to give the command "Crate." What you're after is to get the puppy to go immediately into its crate on command.

A crate-trained dog will obey the "Crate" command eventually whether it's a crate or a strange vehicle you want it to enter.

One woman proved this when one of her Danes was wanted for a commercial showing the proper way to cross-tie a dog in the back of a pickup truck. The Dane, Pinocchio, had never been in the back of a pickup and was not eager to begin. However, at the

"Crate" command, he shrugged his shoulders and hopped in—a strange crate, but to him, a crate, apparently.

The crate-trained puppy who is still in the chewing stage can be left at home safely for a couple of hours (time for you to go to a movie, for instance, or on a shopping trip to replace all the stuff it has chewed up). Inside the crate, your pup will even be happy—and your house is safe.

Cat Crates, Too

Kittens, too, need and appreciate the safety of their own crate, though the cat crate needs to be more private than the dog crate. If you take your kitten on car trips with you, being accustomed to a crate makes the whole matter much more feasible and less stressful for the cat.

The same approach that one uses on pups works with kittens. Put the pet in the crate, keeping the door open for a while, pet the kitten and reassure it, then work up to closing the door. Kittens, being ever so curious about small, enclosed places, will check out a crate thoroughly and accept it without too much urging from you.

If you have visitors, especially small children, who pester your pup or kitten, the crate becomes your pet's place of escape.

Until you've lived with a crate, you may tend to view it as unwarranted restriction. Later, you'll wonder, "How did I ever live without crates before?" On show trips, many dogs prefer their crates to riding loose in the vehicle. Because they're away from home for long times, their crate is their home-away-from-home.

Not Punishment

One final word: Don't use the crate as punishment, or you'll cause your pet to dislike it. Yes, you can, when you're fed up with everyone, send your pet to its crate. If your dogs are like many, they'll learn to notice when your mood blackens and beat you to the draw.

One night when a pet owner was at odds with the whole world, she dropped a pan while getting supper. It was the last straw, and she was ready to blow up when she heard a banging and thumping from the crate near her in the kitchen. Checking, she saw two noses peer out of a crate she considered large enough only for a puppy—her two house dogs had zipped into their safe spot and were cautiously peeking out to see what she was doing. She reports that her black mood left immediately when she saw that silly sight. But you can see how a crate becomes a haven.

Toys

Every young being likes to play. Indeed, nothing can cheer you up, after the pain of watching a pet get old and die, like a silly puppy or a zany kitten dashing around with its toys. However, just as people don't give human babies dangerous toys, so we must be sure our pets' toys won't hurt them.

Teething puppies need something of their own to gnaw on, and many people believe that rawhide bones are about the best things you can give them. This isn't true. The leather softens when it gets wet, gets slippery, and pieces can stick in the pup's throat. Veterinarians have seen many dogs choke on rawhide, and some pets have died. Instead, give the harder, plastic bones that don't get chewed up or stuck. Very large, raw beef bones are good, but don't give cooked bones, as sharp splinters from them can puncture a pup's intestines and cause death. Puppy biscuits are a good choice, too.

If you want to teach your pup to play ball, look for a solid ball made of English rubber. If the ball isn't labeled, you can tell by sniffing. English rubber smells like vanilla. These balls are virtually indestructible.

Avoid jingle balls; the bells come out and pretty soon it's the puppy, not the ball, that's jingling. If you absolutely must have a jingle ball, make sure the pup plays with it only under your supervision.

Tug-of-war toys are fun for you and your pup, as are Frisbees. Keep in mind that no toy should be made of something that will splinter, break, and cause intestinal problems when pieces are swallowed.

Kittens can be started early playing with their own scratching post. This toy will enable them to exercise their natural instincts and will save your furniture. The combination scratching-post-jungle-gym apparatuses keep kittens busy for hours.

Toys that roll and make noise are safe for kittens, as they don't chomp their toys the way puppies do. And kittens, with the exception of clawing the furniture, tend to find things to play with and chase that are non-destructive, unlike puppies. An empty paper bag and a ball of aluminum foil will keep a kitten busy for hours.

Bones are as controversial for kittens as they are for puppies. Whatever you decide, bear in mind that raw bones are safer than cooked ones.

SPAYING
—— AND NEUTERING ——

During your first year with your new pet, you need to decide whether you're going to spay or neuter it. The arguments in favor far outweigh the arguments against, unless you're seriously breeding pure-bred cats or dogs. The neutered male, cat or dog, stays home, doesn't fight, and isn't bothered by the tempting aromas of a female in heat five miles away. The spayed female isn't vulnerable to being bred by every male around, doesn't have to be penned securely or kenneled twice a year, and doesn't have the risks of uterine infections or mammary tumors.

A talk with your veterinarian may convince you that spaying or neutering is the best course of action for your pet.

Interestingly, cats that have been spayed or neutered don't compete in shows against cats that haven't been because it's considered unfair competition. The former are generally in so much better condition than the breeding cats that they just bloom.

—— FOLLOWING YEARS ——

Once you get your pet through its first year, for the next several years exercise and good nutrition should suffice. Of course, a safe, healthy environment is a requirement. Pay attention to the teeth, ears, and any digestive upsets, and get any problems corrected immediately. Don't waste valuable time in the hope that an ear infection will go away or the tartar will disappear by magic. These things use up vital energy that could better be used in generating enthusiasm for a game of ball or a run in the park.

There is very little that should need to be done medically, with the exceptions of scheduled shots, accidents, and passing illnesses. In the early years, you are concerned with prevention of problems that would require treatment if allowed to persist. The main area relating to the prevention of problems is good nutrition. The other major area that's often neglected is the pet's teeth. As we've said earlier, keep those teeth free from tartar.

As your pet starts entering the senior years, approximately seven to ten years old, depending on the pet, start a regular program of physical exams complete with blood tests and X-rays if indicated by your veterinarian. You should have a good working relationship by this time.

By following something similar to the plan we've laid out, you should be able to allow your pet to live up to its genetic capacity for a long time. This will enable it to be healthy and happy and just might take a bit of the anxiety out of your own life, too.

Have confidence in yourself, educate yourself, use all the human resources that are available to you, and enjoy the time you have with your pet to the fullest extent possible.

APPENDIX

Resources

Here's a listing of books or pamphlets to read, as well as companies and organizations to write to for further information.

The subject of pets seems inexhaustible, so this is by no means a complete reference section. It is, rather, an idiosyncratic spectrum of information the authors have found useful.

American Holistic Veterinary Medical Association
2214 Old Emmorton Rd.
Bel Air, MD 21014

Cornucopia Natural Pet Foods
Veterinary Nutritional Assoc., Inc.
229 Wall St.
Huntington, NY 11743

Feed the Kitty—Naturally
Joan Harper
Rt. 3
Richland Center, WI 53581

The Healthy Cat and Dog Cook Book
Joan Harper
(E.P. Dutton, New York, 1979)

International Veterinary Acupuncture Society
RD #4, Box 216
Chester Springs, PA 19425

Keep Your Pet Healthy the Natural Way
Pat Lazarus
Keats Publishing, Inc.
Box 876, New Canaan, CT 06840

The Complete Herbal Handbook for the Dog and Cat
Juliette de Bairadi Levy
Arco Publishing, Inc.
215 Park Ave. South
New York, NY 10003

Lick Your Chops
50 Water St.
South Norwalk, CT 06854

Man Meets Dog
Konrad Lorenz
(Penguin Books, 1965)

National Center for Homeopathy
1500 Massachusetts Ave. NW, Suite 42
Washington, D.C. 20005

Natural Life Pet Products, Inc.
PO Box 476
Maple Plain, MN 55359
Natural Health for Dogs & Cats
Richard H. Pitcairn, DVM, & Susan Hubble Pitcairn
Rodale Press, Emmaus, PA., 1982

Dog Obedience Training
Milo Pearsall and Charles G. Leedham
Charles Scribner's Sons, New York

PetLine
1-800-334-PETS

INDEX

A

Additives. *See under* Diet
Aging and size, in dogs, 9–10
Aging, symptoms of, 5
  cardiovascular system, 44
  digestive system, 33–34
  musculoskeletal system, 51–53
  nervous system, 60
  reproductive system, 58
  respiratory system, 46
  sensory organs, 62–63
  skin, coat and nails, 40
  teeth, 39
  urinary system, 49
Air conditioning, 107
Alfalfa tablets, 96
Anal sacs, 34
Anemia, 126
Anorexia, 101, 117
Antibiotics, 101
Antifreeze, 105
Appetite loss, 36, 63, 136
Arthritis, 53–55, 61, 124, 126
Artificial insemination, 59
Asbestos, 105–106

B

Bad breath, 33, 39, 49
Baths, 41
Bills, veterinarian, 29
Bladder stones, 50–51, 109
Bloating, 34–35, 147
Blood vessels, 45

Bonding with puppy, 150
Bones
  in diet, 99
  healing with comfrey, 126
  as treats, 158, 159
Breathing, difficulty in, 23
Bronchitis, 48
Brushing, 42, 48–49
Burial, 137

C

Calcium, 147–148
Cancer, 37, 48, 53, 114
Carbohydrates, 87
Cardiovascular system, 23, 43–46
Carrying case, 26, 155–158
Cars, 81
Cataracts, 63
Catnip, 98–99
Children
  and death of pet, 136–137
  and old pets, 82
Chills and drafts, 151
Chocolate, 118
Clipping, 43, 44
Coat, 40–43
Cod liver oil, 147
Collars, 153–154
  See also under Flea collars
Comfort, 56
Constipation, 33, 34
Convulsions. *See under* seizures
Corn, 94, 147
Coughing, 44, 48
Crates, 74–75, 155–158
Cysts, 40

D

Deafness, 62–63, 124
Death, signs of approaching, 135–136
Diabetes, 36, 101
Diarrhea, 23, 33, 36, 117, 148
  special diet for, 101
Diet
  additives, 147–148
  amount, 148–149
  bones in, 99
  by-products, 94
  canned foods, 98
  chocolate, 118
  corn and soybeans, 94, 147
  dietary tips, 99–100
  fad diets, 87–89
  fish, 96, 100
  flea control, 110
  fresh food, 91
  greens, 98, 100
  home cooking, 99
  labels, 88, 91–93
  meat, 98
  nutrients, 86–87, 99
  pregnancy, 140
  problems with pet foods, 89, 90
  raw foods, 96–98
  special diets, 100–102
  supplements, 94–99, 141, 147–148
  treats, 102
Digestive system, 33–38
Diseases.
  See also under names of diseases
  emergencies, 22–23
  immunization, 142–146
  symptoms of, 14
Doghouses. *See under* Shelter
Drafts and chills, 151

E

Emergency guidelines, 21–23
Euthanasia, 129–138
  decision to, 136–138
  injections, 137
  and veterinarian, 133–134, 136–137
Exercise, 44–45, 51, 149–150
Exercise pen, 71–72, 152–153
Exterminators, 108–109
Extra-low-frequency fields, 114–115
Eyesight, 63

F

Fats (nutrients), 86–87
Fighting, 83
Fish in diet, 96, 100
Fistulas, 124
Flea collars, 113, 144
Fleas, 41–42, 95, 110–111, 144
Floors, slippery, 72–73
Food. *See under* Diet
Food dish, 73

G

Gastric torsion, 34–35
Gastrointestinal system, 23
Granulomas, 62
Grooming, 40–42

H

Hair balls, 48–49, 125
Harness, 71
Hearing loss, 62–63, 124
Heart, 45, 46
Heartworms, 45–46
Heat, 81
Heatstroke, 44
Herbal medicine, 125–127
Herbicides. *See under* Insecticides
High places, 69–71
Homeopathy, 122–124
Housebreaking, 154–155
Hydrogen peroxide, 23, 116
Hypoglycemia, 61
Hypothermia, 117

I

Immunization, 142–146
Incontinence. *See under* Urination
Indigestion, 33
Inflammation, 51, 53
Insecticides, 104–105, 108–109, 110
    See also under Poisoning
Intestinal parasites. *See under* Parasites

K

Kennels, 79–80, 81
Kidneys, 49–50

L

Lacerations, 22
Leashes, 26, 71, 153–154
Lick granulomas, 62
Life span, 9–10
Litter box, 78, 155
Liver, 37–38
Lungs, 46–48
Lyme disease, 111–112, 113

M

Matting, 42
Minerals, 96–97, 109
Mucous, 48, 95
Muscle, 51–53
Musculoskeletal system, 22, 51–57

N

Nails, 40–43, 44
Napping, 74
Nervous system, 22, 59–62
Neuritis, 62
Neutering, 57–58, 159
Nutrition. *See under* Diet

O

Obesity, 56, 101–102

P

Palliation, 121, 123
Pancreas, inflammation of, 35–36
Paper-training, 154–155
Parasites, 36–37
    worming medications, 114, 144
Pesticides. *See under* Insecticides
Pet doors, 77
Pet food. *See under* Diet
Pet food industry, 89–91
Pet ownership, responsibility of
    57–58, 129–130, 150–151
Pet sitters, 80
Pneumonia, 48
Poisoning, 105, 109–110, 115–118
Pregnancy, 140–141
Private places, 74
Prostate, 59
Protein, 86, 98

R

Radon gas, 108
Renal shutdown, 49
Reproductive system, 57–59
Respiratory system, 23, 46–49
Responsible pet ownership, 57–58,
    129–130, 150–151
Rheumatism, 53
Rugs, 107

S

Salivation, excessive, 39, 117
Scratching post, 158–159
Seizures, 22, 60–61
Senility, 60
Sensory organs, 62–63
Shampoo, 41

Shelter
  crates, 74–75, 155–158
  indoor, 74, 151–152
  outdoor, 76–77, 152–153
Size and aging in dogs, 9–10
Skin, 22, 40–43
Sleeping, increase in, 135
Sleeping quarters, 151–152
Slipped disc, 55–56
Slippery floors, 72–73
Smell (sense), 63
Soybeans, 94, 147
Spaying, 159
Spinal cord problems, 61–62, 125
Stairs, 68–69
Stool, 33, 36, 37
Strokes, 61
Swallowing, difficulty in, 39

T

Tapeworm. *See under* Parasites
Tartar, 38, 39
Teeth, 38–39
Teething puppies, 158
Tendonitis, 53
Thyroid, 37
Ticks, 111–113
Toxins. *See under* Poisoning
Toys, 158–159
Travelling, 81
Treats, 102
Tumors, 33, 39, 40, 58

U

Ulcers, 37
Urinary system, 23, 49–51
Urination

blood in urine, 51, 117
frequency, 49
incontinence, 58–59, 60, 62, 77–78,
     117, 124, 135–136
smell on breath, 49
straining during, 50–51
Uterus, 58

V

Veterinarians
  alternative therapies, 119–120
  and children, 25
  choosing, 17–20
  dentistry, 39
  and euthanasia, 133–134, 136–137
  examination by, 143, 144–146
  information needed by, 27–29
  need for pet restraints, 26
  paying bills, 29
  owner and, 24–29, 146
Vitamins, 95–96, 147–148
Vomiting, 23, 33, 109, 117

W

Warts, 40
Water, 36, 109–110
Weight, 56, 101–102
Weight loss, 36, 37
Wheezing, 44
Worms. *See under* Parasites

Z

Zinc ascorbate, 63
Zinc supplements, 96